HOW TO BE INVISIBLE

KATE BUSH

How To Be Invisible

FABER & FABER

First published in the UK in 2018
First published in the USA in 2019
by Faber & Faber Ltd,
Bloomsbury House,
74–77 Great Russell Street,
London WC1B 3DA

Typeset by Faber & Faber Ltd
Printed in Germany by GGP Media GmbH, Pößneck

A CIP record for this book
is available from the British Library

ISBN 978–0–571–35094–0

10 9 8 7 6 5 4 3 2 1

For Bertie

Contents

Introduction

A book of lyrics is a strange beast. Readers who know the songs become 'hearers' as the brain belts out a speeded-up version of the familiar recording, while those readers unfamiliar with the lyrics are confronted by text presented in a poetry format, but which is avowedly not poetry. Poetry is a solo art form: most lyrics need to leave room for, and craft an affinity with, music – just as lines in a screenplay must be sparse enough to allow for an actor's interpretation. Even in instances where lyrics could pass for poetry to the unwary, lyrics on the page are still a boat in dry-dock, removed from the elements that buoy them and determine their velocity. If quoted aloud, they can be susceptible to spoof: the shadow of Peter Sellers reciting 'A Hard Day's Night' in the style of Laurence Olivier's Richard III falls a long way. A book of lyrics, then, begs a question: who would want such a strange beast purring on the bookshelf?

Answers will vary. Mine goes something like, 'Me; if the lyrics are by one of a small handful of artists whose work has enriched my life and mind over decades.' For me, Kate Bush is one of that handful, and I value this perspective on her songs, the way a shipwright would value that dry-dock view of a ship: he or she spots things that a passenger doesn't when the ship is skimming over the waves. To dispense with the metaphors, I've been a fan for nearly forty years. Being a fan, like being in love, is giddying, it's as personal as skin, it connects you with others in a particular way, and it sets you up for a fall. Being a fan puts you on one-way first name terms with the object of your fan-ness, even if he, she, they or 'Kate' don't know you exist – as is almost always the case. Over time, the 'fan-state' may change in expression but not in essence. 'Fan' as a label is a slur on your critical objectivity and even your maturity, but if you weren't a fan of something or someone, wouldn't life be a little bland?

'Bland' was a fair description of my first stab at an introduction for this fine Faber collection of Kate's lyrics. It focused on Kate's use of language and cultural importance, and kept the Kate Bush fan away from my laptop. A few hundred words in, it died of thirst. For this second attempt, then, I'd like to look at the lyrics along with my own memories of Kate's songs and albums, and my growth from boyhood to 'fan-hood'. By doing so, I hope to shed a little light on why, for millions around the world, Kate is way more than another singer-songwriter: she is a creator of musical companions that travel with you through life. One paradox about Kate is that while her lyrics are proudly idiosyncratic, those same lyrics evoke emotions and sensations that feel universal. Literature works in similar mysterious ways. Kate's the opposite of a confessional singer-songwriter in the mould of Joni Mitchell during her *Blue* period. You don't learn much about Kate from her songs. She's fond of masks and costumes – lyrically and literally – and of yarns, fabulations and atypical narrative viewpoints. Yet, these fiercely singular songs, which nobody else could have authored, are also maps of the heart, the psyche, the imagination. In other words, art.

Pre-YouTube, pre-Spotify, pre-DVD, the predominant TV showcase for pop music was BBC1's *Top of the Pops*. It began life in 1964 and by the late 1970s a show consisted of thirty minutes of acts from that week's Top 30 miming their hits to the studio audience, spliced with pop videos and presented by a pair of BBC Radio DJs. To millennials, *Top of the Pops* may sound as quaint as 1950s radio does to my generation; but most British children of the seventies and eighties will have memories of Thursday evenings in front of the TV, when up to 15 million viewers tuned in. Those of us watching one week in January 1978 saw a video of a ghostly young woman with long black hair, kohl-ringed eyes and red fingernails, dancing her way in a flowing white dress through a song called 'Wuthering Heights'. She mimed the words in a stylised mime-artist manner I'd never seen before; and 'mime-sang' in a swooping, delirious, octave-straddling voice that I'd never heard. Who was she? What was she? Why did she dance like that? Why were there sometimes two, sometimes three of her? What were those lyrics? A pop song about an Emily Brontë novel? At school the following morning all the girls at my small rural primary school were dancing around the schoolyard like twenty Kate Bushes, irrespective of body-shape or size, trailing half-remembered lyrics and clouds of frosted breath. I remember our headmaster watching from the school steps, his jaw open and his thought-bubble reading, 'In thirty-five years of teaching, I've never seen the like of this.' Stories of bishops receiving calls from primary schools asking for a mass exorcism sound far-fetched, but fiction can be truer than truth. The following week, 'Wuthering Heights' knocked ABBA's 'Take a Chance on Me' off the singles chart's number one perch. 'Wuthering Heights' was the first ever song written by a female artist to top the charts; a female artist, in Kate's case, who was only eighteen years old when she wrote it.

Other than *Top of the Pops*, the only ways to access music were the radio, record shops or friends. Then as now, radio was a lucky dip with many more misses than hits. Buying an actual LP represented a major risk when pocket money was 30p a week and an album cost £5. Understandably, shops had no-returns policies and listening booths had been phased out by my record-buying days. If an album you bought turned out to be a turkey with only one good single on it when you got it home, this was a medium-sized tragedy: you could only buy three or four in a year. Risk encouraged conservatism. You stuck to LPs heard in friends' bedrooms; and nobody in my home-taping circle owned either of Kate's first two albums, *The Kick Inside* and 1978's follow-up *Lionheart*. I heard, and loved, Kate's precocious teen-dream 'The Man with the Child in His Eyes', but had no means to hear it again. It haunted me for years. I was luckier with 'England My Lionheart'. One night I was listening to DJ Annie Nightingale under the blankets when Kate's unmistakable voice came on: I fumbled over to my shoebox-sized cassette recorder, pressed PLAY and RECORD and, by holding the radio's speaker against the built-in mike, managed to capture about two-thirds of the song. I was, and am, entranced by this song's Baroque-tinted, concertina-ing of English history, in which a personified, beloved England is 'Dropped from my black Spitfire to my funeral barge'. Nine words encompass five hundred years, and an early example of how time can be compressed or ductile in Kate's lyrics.

Luckily, my brother had both a three-year advantage in purchasing power, and a fondness for Kate. He bought the vinyl LP of *Never for Ever* in late 1980. I pored over its every detail like I would later pore over my first (and last) love-letter. Its cover art was an illustration of monsters and animals streaming out from under Kate's skirt, and bore a frisson of the profane, the pagan and Sheela na gig carvings. Its songs were shot through with sounds I'd heard rarely or never heard: Prophet synthesisers, a fretless bass, drum-machines, a prismatic vocal stack on 'Night Scented Stock'. The lyrics, too, were like nothing else. 'Babooshka' is a miniature short story about a woman initiating adultery with her own husband. 'Delius' is her first 'character study' song about the composer, viewed through the lens of his amanuensis Eric Fenby's memoir. Who, prior to 1980, put a song on a pop album about a classical composer? The song 'Violin' is an unruly cousin of *The Kick Inside*'s suaver 'Saxophone'. 'The Infant Kiss', haunted by shades from *The Turn of the Screw* and the film James's novel inspired, describes a governess falling for a small boy possessed by the spirit of *un homme fatale*. In the waltz 'Army Dreamers' Kate sings the role of a mother burying her soldier son and wondering why he hadn't been a guitarist – no money – or a politician – no education – or a father – he didn't reach his twenties. It's a crisp description of how opportunities in life are bestowed or denied by social background. For me, the most arresting song on the album is its closing track, 'Breathing', in which Kate channels a sentient foetus at the outbreak of a nuclear war. The first half of the song is a kind of seance, not with the dead, but with the not-yet-born. Lyrically, 'Breathing' was Kate's most mature work to date. I like the glinting internal rhymes and the kindergarten-sinister verb in 'Chips of Plutonium are twinkling in every lung'. In part two, a voice describes a nuclear explosion and a looping chorus is sung by Roy Harper, who may be the foetus's father, or the voice of the world. The 'we' in *'What are we going to do without?'* could be the couple and their unborn child facing a nuclear winter; or it could be a question for Homo sapiens, inventor of its own means of annihilation. Overall, *Never for Ever* still stands today as a Cabinet of Curiosities housing some highly desirable items. Its lyrics are variously sensuous, brainy, playful, earnest, twilit and magpie-minded. It never lapses into cliché. If the album has no overall unifying theme beyond an imaginative fertility that birthed its songs, it certainly doesn't suffer for it. By this point in her young career Kate had already wearied of promotional tours, yet despite minimal publicity, *Never for*

Ever debuted on the British album charts at the number one position. It was the first studio album by a solo female artist ever to reach that position at all; let alone during the week of its release.

Far from resting on *Never for Ever*'s laurels, Kate rewove those laurels into her first masterpiece: 1982's majestic, haywire and widdershins *The Dreaming*. The album's first track, 'Sat in Your Lap', is a statement of intent and serves as a stylistic overture: a relentless polyrhythm glory whose meaning – about truth's ultimate slipperiness – is itself slippery. The LP requires multiple plays for its beauties to emerge fully. It is as far from being 'Wuthering Heights' as it could be, while still being Kate Bush. The album is never painterly, like *Never for Ever* frequently is. Orchestration is absent. The songs are tense, headlong and overlain and sometimes filtered through accents. They lull and startle with wild dynamic swings. The album's sound has something of the artful post-punk asperity of Peter Gabriel's third album, on which Kate sings; and the diced-and-sliced feel of David Byrne and Brian Eno's *My Life in the Bush of Ghosts*. Lyrically, the songs are febrile lucid dreams. Even the saner songs, like 'Leave It Open', are shaken by the Stephen King-shaded 'Get Out of My House' – 'The Infant Kiss' with violence – half-sung, half-howled by a poltergeist. Narrative arcs are not neat. Does the smuggler's woman in 'Night of the Swallow' really 'let the law know' about him, or was it just a threat to keep him at home? Who dies at the end of the dark 'Pull Out the Pin' – the Vietnamese soldier or the big pink hash-smoking American GI; or both? What exactly is the 'gaffa' in 'Suspended in Gaffa'? A private word for a state of limbo or is it just heavy-duty adhesive gaffa-tape?

My brother bought *The Dreaming* on cassette, but the tape was ingested by the ghetto blaster before I'd fully explored the album, and I didn't own my own copy of *The Dreaming* until I was living in Japan in the late 1990s. I listened to it on repeat as I worked on my first two novels. *The Dreaming* became a kind of sonic amulet; an order to take the road less travelled. A line like, 'See the light ram through the gaps in the land' from the title track would swim into focus as I wrote, and I'd think, That's glorious: try to choose words that do that . . . Years later, I still unearth new things in the album's ten songs. I've had the album on repeat as I've written this paragraph and notice for the first time the troubled strangeness of 'All The Love's first line: 'The first time I died . . .' Is that reincarnation? Ripples of *la petite mort*? A soul looking down on its death bed? An unwillingly unreliable narrator who only knows for sure that the love and tears of his soon-to-be bereaved are all in vain, and all too late . . .

The planets aligned for 1985's *Hounds of Love,* released after Kate's first proper break from the industry. She recorded this evergreen masterpiece at a more leisurely pace in her home-studio. It landed in the Live Aid summer like fresh air at the end of long-haul flight. The first side's quintet of songs are rich in melodic oomph, vocal overlays, sonic effects, samples, Fairlight synthesisers that are somehow ageless, a cello and a string ensemble. Kate's voice had ripened. The lyrics were still cliché-free, still uniquely Kate, but less enigmatic and more user-friendly than on *The Dreaming.* 'The Big Sky' is about being a kid and finding shapes in clouds. 'Mother Stands for Comfort' portrays a psychotic murderer who knows his mother knows; and knows that, 'Mother will stay Mum'. 'Cloudbusting' is drawn from Peter Reich's memoir about his father, Wilhelm Reich, the philosopher/psychologist/pseudoscientist (take your pick and don't troll me) and inventor of an alleged rain-making machine. The lyrics deal less with the great man himself than with a son's realisation that his father has feet of clay; and how that realisation informs filial love. 'Hounds of Love' is another 'typically atypical' Kate love song addressed not to the beloved but to the fear of love and the dangers it engenders. Images and symbols pound by at the speed of an elevated heartbeat: the eponymous hounds; an 'It' in the trees, coming for you; a fox cub cradled in your elbow; taking off shoes, and thrrrrrrowing them in the lake. First amongst equals is perhaps 'Running Up That Hill', whose original title 'A Deal With God' was bracketed off by EMI to avoid offending Catholic theocracies. The song posits that God (not the Devil, for an extra spoonful of subversion) allows a woman and her male lover to swap bodies during sex and 'exchange the experience'. 'Running Up That Hill' is a thumping, stormy, sacred-and-profane, frankly orgasmic tryst of a song. Not only the most bewitchingly, persuasive and naked song about sex that I'd ever heard; it was also the first song I'd encountered that validated female sexual pleasure as distinct from its male counterpoint. Which, in an important sense, made it my first taste of feminism in popular art.

In 1985, female autonomy in the arts was groundbreaking. Kate's example was surely encouraging for young women, and instructive for hundreds of thousands of young straight middle-class British males my age. Did we all go on to establish a post-feminist Utopia in which both sexes no longer tolerate the squandering of human talent and the damage to relationships caused by a smug patriarchy? Demonstrably not. Was 'Hounds of Love' a first encounter with a new gender consciousness for many, me included? Well, believe it or not, in a way, yes. Was Kate Bush a one-woman answer to the question, 'Where are all the real female artists in music, then?' God Yes.

Side two of *Hounds of Love* is a song-cycle of seven linked songs entitled *The Ninth Wave* about a woman's struggle for survival floating alone in the sea at night. I liked it even more than the masterclass of songwriting on side one. For me, *The Ninth Wave* glints with Schubert's *Winterreise*, recalls loose 1960s concept albums like the Beatles' *Sgt. Pepper's Lonely Hearts Club Band* and a few 1970s prog-rock narratives; but *The Ninth Wave* is, once again, its own sublime Kate-esque creation that eschews lazy comparison with anything else in rock/pop. Its sonic palette incorporates piano ballad, Georgian chant, sampling, Irish trad. and sound montage. The story is sketched out in clues. The listener (or reader of the lyrics) is required to work, to guess, to imagine. Is 'And Dream of Sheep's 'little light shining' the light on the life jacket? In 'Under Ice' is there 'not a soul on the ice' because the skater's soul is in fact trapped under the ice? In the hallucinatory 'Waking the Witch', is the woman translating her fight against drowning as a psychodrama of a witch-hunt and subsequent witch-drowning; or is she remembering her death from a former life? The lyrics speak in oxygen-starved obliquenesses, not dry land certainties. The more I listened to *The Ninth Wave*, both in my old bedroom in my parents' house and in a dozen student dorm rooms at college, the more the cycle posed questions. Does the woman even survive? 'The Morning Fog', the final song in the cycle, brings daylight and a vow to cherish loved ones better. Is the protagonist being airlifted to safety, or are they her dying thoughts, as the lines, 'I am falling/ Like a stone' could suggest? Can we trust her words, or has she gone the way of William Golding's drowning sailor Pincher Martin, whose mind conjures into being an imaginary islet whose shape is the shape of a hollow in his tooth? My answers to these questions still shift. *The Ninth Wave* is, like Robert Wyatt's 'Sea Song', different every time.

1987's *The Sensual World* and 1993's *The Red Shoes* strike me as two halves of a diptych. They have in common an array of diverse admirer-collaborators – the Bulgarian singers Trio Bulgarka (who appear on both albums), Prince, Nigel Kennedy, Japan's bassist Mick Karn, David Gilmour and Eric Clapton. Lyrically, they read like two collections of short stories. *The Sensual World* opens with a Molly Bloom-inspired monologue from *Ulysses*: Joyce's estate allowed Kate to use the original for her 2009 re-recording, but not the 1987 version, where Kate substituted her own text. 'A Deeper Understanding' is a prescient tale of alienation in the digital age and a man's love for his computer's operating system. 'Heads We're Dancing' could have been a *Tales of the Unexpected* script back in the day: I won't give away the sting in the tall tale's tail here. The stratospheric 'Rocket's Tail' sees Kate turn into a firework powered by the dynamite of Pink Floyd's Stratocaster; while 'This Woman's Work', one of Kate's most poignant songs, narrates a dangerous birth with an uncertain conclusion. *The Red Shoes* LP, whose title references both the Powell and Pressburger film and Hans Christian Andersen's sinister fairy tale, similarly has one foot in literature and another in cinema; and, similarly, is heady with obsession. The LP's highlights are many. The title track, like the film, depicts the toxic aspects of marriage to art. 'Moments of Pleasure' is a reverie-requiem for Kate's dead, ushered in by one of her most evocative phrases, 'Here come the Hills of Time'. I enjoy the logic-defying flip in the chorus to 'Constellation of the Heart' which declares, 'We take all the telescopes/ And we turn them inside out/. . . And here we'll find the constellation of the heart.' A trio of anguished songs across the album – 'And So Is Love', 'Song of Solomon' and 'You're the One' – describe, in full colour, exactly what the hounds of love are capable of, and what state they'll leave you in, once they've had their way with you. 'You're the One' in particular is perhaps Kate's most hard-won, raw-nerved song.

These two albums stir up emotional sediment; a sense of
the impermanence of things, and a fear that even the recipe
for divine protection served up by Lily in her eponymous
song might not be enough. *The Sensual World* appeared
when I was eking out a student grant, so I had to make
do with a taped copy on a C60 cassette, courtesy of my
brother once again. *Hounds of Love* and Kate's greatest-hits
collection *The Whole Story* was in many a late 1980s student
bedroom, but *The Sensual World* was less common, and when
this cassette also got mangled, that was that. I was even more
broke six years later when *The Red Shoes* came out, living a
'rent insecure' existence in London with no more possessions
than would fit into a backpack. A flatmate who worked for
music magazine *Smash Hits* got a promotional CD featuring
'Moments of Pleasure'; but when that flat fell through, Kate
was gone. As with *The Dreaming*, I went exploring inside *The
Sensual World* and *The Red Shoes* only when I was living in
Hiroshima a few years later, by which point I had a few hard-
won, raw-nerved experiences of my own. What else are your
twenties for?

After *The Red Shoes*, Kate released nothing. Year upon
year of it. Not just no new music – no interviews, no TV
appearances, no *This Is Your Life*, no place-marking *Kate
Bush Unplugged*. No official 'Kate Bush has retired from
show-business' statement. Was there a precedent for this?
Certainly, music careers ended and artists were dropped by
their labels; usually after a couple of poorly judged albums
and a 're-invention', doomed by a lack of invention in the
first place. This wasn't true of Kate. Even when she wasn't
in the media or releasing material, she was still referred to
as an eminent British recording artist. Her back catalogue
continued to sell, to be played, and to be cherished. Her
critical cachet and (what was now called a) fanbase kept

growing as her albums made their own way in the world, and found their way into the Walkmans, Discmans and MP3 players of kids young enough to have been conceived to 'Wuthering Heights'. But there was no new news. Pre social media, Kate-fanciers didn't even have baseless rumours to dine on. My generation, who had gaped in astonishment at 'Wuthering Heights', now had jobs, mortgages and children. The longest gap between albums – six years, between *The Sensual World* and *The Red Shoes* – was matched, passed, and left in the dust. I still played everything from *Never for Ever* onwards, several times a year, and I still put on *The Dreaming* to write to, and marvelled at *Hounds of Love*. Where there's life, there's hope, up to a point, and as the ten-year anniversary of *The Red Shoes* came and went, I had to accept the possibility that the last song of Kate's discography would be the bleak song of farewell to a lover she can't live without but can't live with, 'You're the One'.

In 2005, CDs and DVDs still sold in sufficient quantities for HMV to pay rent in Heathrow Airport terminals, and as I passed through on my way home, groggy from red-eye flight, I saw an orange cover of a sky, a sea, an island mountain that looked like a sound wave, and, in an understated size and font, three words, *Aerial*, Kate and Bush. Not just a single album, either: a double. Hallelujah. I'd heard a single, 'King of the Mountain', slightly snootily reviewed a week or so before on BBC Radio 4's *Front Row* with the should-be-immortal verdict – 'It's only got three chords!' – so finding *Aerial* wasn't totally unexpected. Nonetheless, I was still so excited that I left my passport at the till, had to rush back for it from the boarding queue and only just made my flight home to Ireland. I played *Aerial* on a summer's evening in the garden shed that I liked to call my writer's hut. Analogue natives know how the first listen of a subsequently beloved album remains in the memory, vivid and clear; and some of this continued into the CD era. I can still get back to that evening when I play *Aerial*, which I do a few times a year. The double LP was no 'return to form' or a 'comeback album': Kate had never lost her form and, at least to her fans, her music had never gone anywhere. My view of *Aerial* was widely shared: it is Kate's third masterpiece, along with *The Dreaming* and *Hounds of Love*. What constitutes a 'masterpiece' is only established by the ultimate critic, Time; but even producing three contenders for the title in a single career puts a songwriter in the most exclusive company. The traditional canon might offer up The Beatles, The Stones, Bob Dylan, Paul Simon, Joni Mitchell, Radiohead – and, with *Aerial*, Kate Bush.

Disc one of *Aerial*, entitled *A Sea of Honey*, is a portrait gallery in song and lyric. Album opener 'King of the Mountain' is a refugee song from *The Red Shoes* sessions and injects Elvis Presley with a vial of Citizen Kane to portray the psychic derangement of fame. 'Joanni' is a portrait of a woman in the male world of war: Joan of Arc, who 'blows a kiss to God/ And she never wears a ring on her finger', wages a battle over who gets to define her femininity; and, like Kate, wins. 'Pi', omitted from this anthology as even Kate's fans might quail at all the numbers, portrays a mathematician and love of the infinite number. Kate sings the number to tens of decimal places with the tenderness and passion of a lover singing their beloved's name. 'Bertie' is a madrigal about Kate's young son, whose birth and upbringing accounted in no small part for the twelve-year hiatus. By now my wife and I had a small child of our own whose toothy grin was for us, too, 'The most truly fantastic smile/ I've ever seen'. 'Mrs Bartolozzi', surely the only song by a major artist whose lyrics include washing machine onomatopoeia, portrays a housekeeper of a certain age. The drudgery of her life smothers her own memories and desires, and puts me in mind of a twenty-first century Miss Kenton from Kazuo Ishiguro's *The Remains of the Day*. The song 'How To Be Invisible', which I'll shoehorn into my portrait gallery if it kills me, contains a *Macbeth*-esque recipe for invisibility which is, Kate-ishly, both quotidian and magical: 'Eye of Braille/ Hem of Anorak/ Stem of Wallflower/ Hair of Doormat.' Corridors within a fractal labyrinth not only twist and turn but 'blister and burn' as if we're trapped inside a burning photograph or film reel. Disc one's last song is my desert island Kate song: 'A Coral Room'. Musically, this ballad for piano and vocal is one of Kate's sparsest. Lyrically, it's one of her richest, describing an underwater city, dreamy and abandoned and swaying and recalling Debussy's prelude *La Cathédrale engloutie*. The city is deep memory, crawled over by the spider of time, perhaps from 'Moments of Pleasure's hills of time. Speedboats fly above and planes – perhaps a black Spitfire or two – come crashing down. A broken jug contains a memory of Kate's mother and the time the jug broke. After countless plays, I still find it shudderingly beautiful.

Disc two of *Aerial* reprises the song-cycle, though *A Sky of Honey* has no unifying character like the woman adrift in the sea at night in *The Ninth Wave*. It's a morning-to-morning book of hours whose plot is the changing quality of light, the spin of the planet, Nature the Artist and the nature of art, 'Oh will you come with us to find/ The song of the oil and the brush?' A painter makes a mistake – 'That bit there, it was an accident/ But he's so pleased/ It's the best mistake he could make.' Metamorphosis and synaesthesia of colour and sound repeats throughout the cycle. Rain falls on a pavement painting. Night drains the sunset. 'This is a song of colour/ Where sands sing in crimson, red and rust/ Then climb into bed and turn to dust'. The album appeared about six weeks before our son did, and I persuaded myself that

'Spaceboy' (as we referred to him them) was Kate's youngest ever fan, judging by his uterine kicks.

A mere six years later, *50 Words for Snow* was released. It followed only months after *Director's Cut*, an album of re-imagined re-cuts of songs from *The Sensual World* and *The Red Shoes*. This being the social media age, *50 Words for Snow* was forecast before it 'dropped', as our children's generation say without quotes. It is Kate's fourth masterpiece. The songs are expansive, loose-fitting and jazzier in feel than the rest of the oeuvre, thanks to Kate's lower register and huskier vocal cords, plus veteran session drummer Steve Gadd whose percussive lexicon shifts from spacious to flurrying to ominous to trip-hoppy, according to the song's slant. Lyrically, *50 Words for Snow* is themed around winter: a Janus-head opposite to the summer-pollenated *A Sky of Honey*. The album opens with 'Snowflake', a slow and shimmering duet between a falling snowflake 'born in a cloud' and a person destined to catch it. Because the snowflake is voiced and sung by Kate's son and the person by Kate; or maybe because of the small-ish children then in my life, I think of 'Snowflake' also as a duet between a soul before conception (one of multitudes of multitudes) and that soul's new body's future mother. Its lyrics are both primordial – 'I am ice and dust and light/ I am sky and here' – and intimate – 'I think I can see you/ There's your long, white neck.' 'Lake Tahoe' is a ghost story of sorts, featuring a drowned woman in Victorian dress 'tumbling like a cloud that has drowned in the lake' calling for her dog, Snowflake; and that same, now-elderly dog's dream, in which his drowned mistress is still alive. The third song, 'Misty', stars a kind of priapic Raymond Briggs snowman. A woman makes a snowman-lover, spends the night with him, wakes to find, 'The sheets are soaking/ And on my pillow:/ Dead leaves, bits of twisted branches/ And frozen garden'. She half-loses her mind, and (in an echo of Cathy in 'Wuthering Heights') suspects he's out there in the snow, and comes out on the ledge . . . Kate leaves it to us to decide whether the narrative is a Neo-Neo-Gothic fantasy or a fable about the brief expiry date of passion and the corrosive hunger for more it leaves after melting away. The subject of 'Wild Man' is the Yeti; the narrator (slightly reminiscent of 'Pulling Out the Pin') is a 'native' Himalayan who knows the Yeti is no langur monkey, no big brown bear; and knows what hunters will do to the Wild Man if they find him. He or she brushes away the footprints. 'Snowed In at Wheeler Street' outdoes 'England My Lionheart' by magicking 1700 years of history into the top hat of a couple of verses. Two star-crossed lovers recount joint-memories of previous meetings at the sacking of Rome, on steps in revolutionary Paris, on opposing sides of a Partisan War in 1942, during the London smog, on 9/11 in New York. Are they conditional immortals? Are they serial reincarnatees? (I was writing a novel populated by both categories when *50 Words for Snow* was released, and this song made my book feel less fantastical and more possible.) The lovers are united in the song, and perhaps in an earlier decade, Kate would have left them there: but the song ends in a maturer person's 'And now what?' The snow will melt, they'll have to leave, and 'I'd live that day over and over/ But the world won't stop turning'. Time wins again. The title track is a blizzard of fifty haiku-dense Joyce-esque words for snow minted by Kate (except for the Klingon), spoken by Stephen Fry on the recording, and by my Stephen-Fry-of-the-mind when I read this book. My favourites vary, though 'Wenceslasaire', 'shovelcrusted' and 'blown from polar fur' never let me down. 'Among Angels' is a delicate closer of mirrors and angels, inviting you to 'Lay your broken laugh at their feet.' That the broken noun is not 'heart' but 'laugh' is a last-minute cliché-sidestep characteristic of Kate. By giving substance to something fleeting and immaterial – a laugh – it is made breakable; and, therefore, fixable, curable and lasting. The song's last, contrapuntal word, is 'Summer'.

At the time of writing, *50 Words for Snow* is Kate's last studio album. Millions of Kate's fans around the world hope more albums will join it, thus requiring expanded reprints of this anthology in future. As a bonus in this edition, however, lyrics are included from many of Kate's B-sides and non-album tracks. Some of these song are as accomplished as many a songwriter's career-bests. 'You Want Alchemy' is a *Red Shoes*-era musical jaunt about bees and a beekeeper whose lyrics tongue-in-cheekily plant Kate Bush next to The Beatles – 'On a cloudbusting kind of day/ We took our own Mystery Tour' – before veering into the demotic: 'And we're thinking/ Who is this guy?/ Is he some kind of nut or what?' This insolently long introduction hasn't really touched on Kate's humour, but it's here, there and everywhere to be relished. To my mind, the cut and polished diamond of these compositions is 'Under the Ivy', a short song from the *Hounds of Love* era. I can't help but interpret it as a kind of self-portrait or 'meta-song' about the Kate and her oeuvre which has existed 'away from the party' of musical fashion since the start of her career. Her music is secluded 'under the ivy' and yet it invites you to join it, almost coyly: 'It wouldn't take me long/ To tell you how to find me . . .' Both Kate's wariness of celebrity and her oneness with music and sound are recalled by the lines, 'I sit here in the thunder/ The green on the grey/ I feel it all around me/ And it's not easy for me/ To give away a secret/ It's not safe.' Yet Kate does give away secrets. She encodes them into extraordinary songs like this one.

*

Across the zoology of artists, age exerts itself unequally. The odds of poets, playwrights, visual artists, composers and musicians having fertile 'late careers' are pretty good. Actors, too, can mature into greatness, provided the right parts come along. Film-makers and novelists are somewhere in the middle: there's no clear reason why they shouldn't create work in their fifties or sixties that's as vital and illuminating as the work from their thirties; and some do; but more don't. The average career-length of recording artists, however, makes footballers look long-lived. It's as if what makes them popular – that effortless harmony with the zeitgeist – is what condemns them to obsolescence once that zeitgeist has floated off elsewhere. It's not that they forget to write songs; it's just that the new songs no longer make the hairs on the back of your neck rise. Fans, too, can be the most fair-weather of friends. We want more of what we loved the first time, yet we complain if things feel repetitive. Kate is a mighty exception to all this, as rare as a real live yeti. Her fidelity to her ever-curious, ever-morphing muse has won her a global legion of devotees for whom her songs are treasured possessions, infused with private memories, to be carried through life. By dint of never having been in fashion, Kate has never fallen out of fashion. By taking bold artistic risks, which she navigates with ingenuity and wisely chosen collaborators, the albums Kate made in her late forties and fifties equal and surpass the songs recorded in her teens and twenties that made her famous. To any artist in any field, her example is a hope-instilling exhortation to evolve, to re-invent, to re-imagine what we do. This is why I'll be keeping this strange beast, *How To Be Invisible*, on my bookshelf for the rest of my days.

David Mitchell
West Cork, 2018

Author's Note

A few of the lyrics in this book were originally released as B-sides for singles and so have never appeared in print before.

'Lyra' was written for the end titles of the film *The Golden Compass*.

'A Sky of Honey' includes 'Tawny Moon', which was specially written for the Before the Dawn live shows. Also included are some extended lyrics that were created because of visual content that took place on stage.

All the lyrics have been reviewed as works of verse without their music and so in some places are more detailed than how they originally appeared on the albums.

I found a book on
how to be invisible...

Snowflake

I was born in a cloud . . .
Now I am falling
I want you to catch me
Look up and you'll see me
You know you can hear me

The world is so loud
Keep falling
I'll find you

We're over a forest
There's millions of snowflakes
We're dancing

The world is so loud
Keep falling
And I'll find you

I am ice and dust
I am sky

I can see horses wading through snowdrifts
My broken hearts, my fabulous dances
My fleeting song, fleeting

The world is so loud
Keep falling
I'll find you

My broken hearts, my fabulous dance
My fleeting song
My twist and shout

I am ice and dust and light
I am sky and here

I can hear people.
I think you are near me now

The world is so loud
Keep falling
I'll find you

We're over a forest
It's midnight at Christmas

The world is so loud
Keep falling
I'll find you

I think I can see you
There's your long, white neck

The world is so loud
Keep falling
I'll find you

Now I am falling
Look up and you'll see me

The world is so loud
Keep falling
I'll find you

In a moment or two
I'll be with you

The world is so loud
Keep falling
I'll find you

Be ready to catch me . . .

The world is so loud
Keep falling
I'll find you

Top of the City

One more step to the top of the city
Where just a couple of pigeons are living
Up on the angel's shoulders

I don't know if I'm closer to Heaven but
It looks like Hell down there
These streets have never been
Paved with gold
Welcome to the loneliest city in
The world
It's no good for you baby
It's no good for you now
Keep looking up for the ladder

I don't know if you'll love me for it
But I don't think we should
Suffer this
There's just one thing we can
Do about it

Take me up to the top of the city
Take me up to the top of the city
Take me up to the top of the city
And put me up on the
Angel's shoulders

See how that building there is
Nearly built
There's a big fire over on the north
Of the city

I see you walking down the street
With her
I see your lights going on and off
She's no good for you baby
She's no good for you now
Look I'm here with the ladder

I don't know if you love me or not
But I don't think we should
Ever suffer
There's just one thing we can
Do about this

Take me up to the top of the city
Take me up to the top of the city
Up to the highest point of the city
One more step to the top of the city
Put me up on the angel's shoulders

And I don't mind if it's dangerous
I don't mind if it's raining
Take me up to the top of the city

And put me up on the
Angel's shoulders
Take me up to the top of the city
Mmm yes, one more step to the
Top of the city
And put me up on the
Angel's shoulders

Love and Anger

It lay buried here, it lay deep inside me
It's so deep I don't think that I can
Speak about it
It could take me all of my life
But it would only take a moment to
Tell you what I'm feeling
But I don't know if I'm ready yet.
You come walking into this room
Like you're walking into my arms,
What would I do without you?

Take away the love and the anger
And a little piece of hope holding us together
Looking for a moment that'll never happen
Living in the gap between past and future
Take away the stone and the timber
And a little piece of rope won't hold it together

If you can't tell your sister
If you can't tell a priest
'Cause it's so deep you don't think that you can
Speak about it to anyone . . .
Can you tell it to your heart?
Can you find it in your heart
To let go of these feelings
Like a bell to a Southerly wind
We could be like two strings beating,
Speaking in sympathy . . .
What would we do without you?
Two strings speak in sympathy

Take away the love and the anger
And a little piece of hope holding us together
Looking for a moment that'll never happen
Living in the gap between past and future
Take away the stone and the timber
And a little piece of rope won't hold it together

We're building a house of the future together
(What would we do without you?)
Well, if it's so deep you don't think that you
Can speak about it
Just remember to reach out and touch
The past and the future
Well, if it's so deep you don't think you
Can speak about it
Don't ever think that you can't change
The past and the future
You might not, not think so now
But just you wait and see
Someone will come to help you

The Song of Solomon

The Song of Solomon
The song of everyone
Who walks the path
Of the solitary heart
The soul cries out
Hear a woman singing

Don't want your bullshit, yeah
Just want your sexuality
Don't want excuses, yeah
Write me your poetry in motion
Write it just for me, yeah
And sign it with a kiss

Mmm, just take any line
'Comfort me with apples
For I am sick of love
His left hand is under my head
And his right hand
Doth embrace me'
This is the Song of Solomon
Here's a woman singing

Don't want your bullshit, yeah
Just want your sexuality
Don't want excuses, yeah
Write me your poetry in motion
Write it just for me, yeah
And sign it with a kiss

And I'll do it for you
I'll be the Rose of Sharon for you
I'll do it for you
I'll be the Lily of the Valley for you
I'll do it for you
I'll be Isolde or Marion for you
I'll do it for you
Ooh I'll come in a hurricane for you
I'll do it for you

A wop-bam-boom

Don't want your bullshit, yeah
Just want your sexuality

Hounds of Love

When I was a child
Running in the night
Afraid of what might be
Hiding in the dark
Hiding in the street
And of what was following me
Now hounds of love are hunting
I've always been a coward
And I don't know what's good for me

Here I go
It's coming for me thro' the trees
Help me someone, help me please
Take my shoes off and throw them in the lake
And I'll be two steps on the water

I found a fox caught by dogs
He let me take him in my hands
His little heart, it beats so fast
And I'm ashamed of running away,
From nothing real, I just can't deal with this
I'm still afraid to be there
Among your hounds of love
And feel your arms surround me
I've always been a coward
And never know what's good for me

Here I go, don't let me go
Tie me to the mast
Hold me down

It's coming for me through the trees
Help me darling, help me please
Take my shoes off and throw them in the lake
And I'll be two steps on the water

I don't know what's good for me
I don't know what's good for me
I need love, love, love, love, love, yeah
Your love

Take your shoes off and throw them in the lake
Do you know what I really need?
Do you know what I really need?
I need love, love, love, love, love, yeah

King of the Mountain

Could you see the aisles of women?
Could you see them screaming and weeping?
Could you see the storm rising?
Could you see the guy who was driving?
Could you climb higher and higher?
Could you climb right over the top?
Why does a multi-millionaire
Fill up his home with priceless junk?

The wind is whistling
The wind is whistling
Through the house

Elvis are you out there somewhere
Looking like a happy man?
In the snow with Rosebud
And king of the mountain

Another Hollywood waitress
Is telling us she's having your baby
And there's a rumour that you're on ice
And you will rise again someday
And that there's a photograph
Where you're dancing on your grave

The wind is whistling
The wind is whistling
Through the house

Elvis are you out there somewhere
Looking like a happy man?
In the snow with Rosebud
And king of the mountain

The wind it blows
The wind it blows the door closed

Take a pinch of keyhole
And fold yourself up
You cut along the dotted line...

Cloudbusting

I still dream of Orgonon.
I wake up crying
You're making rain
And you're just in reach
When you and sleep escape me

You're like my yo-yo
That glowed in the dark

What made it special
Made it dangerous
So I bury it and forget

But every time it rains,
You're here in my head
Like the sun coming out
I just know that something good is gonna happen
I don't know when
But just saying it could even make it happen

On top of the world
Looking over the edge
You could see them coming
You looked too small
In their big black car
To be a threat to the men in power

I hid my yo-yo in the garden
I can't hide you from the government
Oh God, Daddy – I won't forget

'Cause every time it rains,
You're here in my head
Like the sun coming out
I just know that something good is gonna happen
I don't know when
But just saying it could even make it happen

Everytime it rains
You're here in my head
Like the sun coming out –
Like your son's coming out
I just know that something good is gonna happen
I don't know when
But just saying it could even make it happen
Ooh just saying it could even make it happen

I'm cloudbusting, Daddy

Your son's coming out
Your sun's coming out.

The Big Sky

They look down at the ground, missing
But I never go in now
I'm looking at the Big Sky
I'm looking at the Big Sky now
I'm looking at the Big Sky
You never understood me.
You never really tried

That cloud, that cloud – looks like Ireland
C'mon and blow it a kiss now
But quick 'cause it's changing in the Big Sky
It's changing in the Big Sky now
We're looking at the Big Sky
You never understood me
You never really tried

This cloud, this cloud says, 'Noah,
C'mon and build me an Ark'
And if you're coming – jump

'Cause we're leaving with the Big Sky
We're leaving with the Big Sky, honey
We're leaving with the Big Sky

Looking at the . . .
We're looking at the . . .

And we pause for the jet

Hup, hup
Hup, in the Big Sky

We're looking at the Big Sky, honey
You want my reply?
Well what's the question? Yeah
I was looking at the Big Sky
. . . Big Sky
Looking at the Big Sky
We're looking at the . . .

Tell me, sisters . . .

Roll over like a great big cloud
Walking out in the Big Sky

You Want Alchemy

What a lovely afternoon
On a cloudbusting kind of day
We took our own Mystery Tour
And got completely lost somewhere up in the hills
And we came upon a beekeeper
And he said, 'Did you know they can change it all?'

You want alchemy?
They turn the roses into gold
They turn the lilac into honey
They're making love for the peaches

And we're thinking
Who is this guy?
Is he some kind of nut or what?
He said, 'I don't meet many people
I'm very busy with the hives
Bzzz, sun's going down
Oh, when's my cloud of bees coming home?'

They got alchemy
They turn the roses into gold
They turn the lilac into honey
They're making love for the peaches
And they'll do it! Do it for you
They'll do it! Do it for you

'And if you see them, send them right on home to me'
What they gonna do?
Turn the roses into gold

And they'll do it for you! Do it for you
What they gonna do?
I'll tell you
They're making love for the peaches
What they gonna do?
Turning lilac into honey
They do it for you
They do it for you
'And why not?
They bring me so much pleasure'

Delius (Song of Summer)

Ooh, he's a moody old man
Song of summer in his hand
Ooh, he's a moody old man
In his hand
In his hand

   'Ta Ta-Ta,
     Hmm
   Ta Ta-Ta'

   Delius
   Delius amat
   Syphilis deus
   Genius, oh

To be sung of a summer
Night on the water
Ooh, on the water –

   'Ta Ta-Ta,
     In B, Fenby!
   Ta Ta-Ta'

   Delius
   Delius amat
   Syphilis deus
   Genius, oh

To be sung of a summer
Night on the water

Ooh, on the water
On the water

Eat the Music

Split me open
With devotion
You put your hands in
And rip my heart out
Eat the music

Does he conceal
What he really feels?
He's a woman at heart
And I love him for that
Let's split him open

Like a pomegranate
Insides out
All is revealed
Not only women bleed

Take the stone out
Of the mango
You put it in your mouth
And pull a plum out

Take a papaya
You like a guava?
Grab a banana
And a sultana
Rip them to pieces
With sticky fingers
Split the banana
Crush the sultana

Split 'em open
With devotion
You put your hands in
And rip their hearts out

Like a pomegranate
Insides out
He's a woman at heart
And love him for that

Take a papaya
You like a guava?
Grab a banana
And a sultana
Rip 'em to pieces
With sticky fingers
Split the banana
Crush the sultana

All emotion
And with devotion
You put your hands in
What ya thinking?
What am I singing?
A song of seeds
The food of love
Eat the music

Bertie

Here comes the sunshine
Here comes that son of mine
Here comes the everything
Here's a song and a song for him

Sweet kisses
Three wishes
Lovely Bertie

The most wilful
The most beautiful
The most truly fantastic smile
I've ever seen

Sweet kisses
Three wishes
Lovely Bertie

You bring me so much joy
And then you bring me
More joy

The Sensual World

Mmh, yes
Then I'd taken the kiss of seedcake back from his mouth
Going deep South, go down, mmh, yes
Took six big wheels and rolled our bodies
Off of Howth Head and into the flesh, mmh, yes
He said I was a flower of the mountain, yes
But now I've powers o'er a woman's body – yes

Stepping out of the page into the sensual world
Stepping out . . .
To where the water and the earth caress
And the down of a peach says mmh, yes
Do I look for those millionaires
Like a Machiavellian girl would?
When I could wear a sunset, mmh, yes
And how we'd wished to live in the sensual world
You don't need words – just one kiss, then another

Stepping out of the page into the sensual world
Stepping out, off the page into the sensual world
And then our arrows of desire rewrite the speech, mmh, yes
And then he whispered would I, mmh, yes
Be safe, mmh, yes, from mountain flowers?
And at first with the charm around him, mmh, yes

He loosened it so if it slipped between my breasts
He'd rescue it, mmh, yes
And his spark took life in my hand and, mmh, yes
I said, mmh, yes

But not yet, mmh, yes
Mmh, yes

Kashka from Baghdad

Kashka from Baghdad
Lives in sin, they say
With another man
But no-one knows who

Old friends never call there
Some wonder if life's
Inside at all –
If there's life inside at all

But we know the lady who rents the room
She catches them calling à la lune

At night
They're seen
Laughing
Loving
They know
The way
To be
Happy

They never go for walks
Maybe it's because
The moon's not bright enough
There's light in love, you see

I watch their shadows
Tall and slim

In the window opposite
I long to be with them

'Cause when all the alley-cats come out
I can hear music from Kashka's house

At night they're seen Laughing, Loving
They know the way to be happy

'Watching every night
Don't you know they're seen?
Won't you let me laugh?
Let me in your love

'Watching every night
Don't you know they're seen?
Won't you let me laugh?
Let me in your love

'Watching every night.
Don't you know they're seen?
Won't you let me laugh?'

Sat in Your Lap

I see the people working, and see it working for them
And so I want to join in, but then I find it hurts me
Some say that knowledge is something sat in your lap
Some say that knowledge is something that you never have
I see the people happy, so can it happen for me?
'Cause when I am unhappy, there's nothing that can move me
Some say that knowledge is something that you never have
Some say that knowledge is something sat in your lap
Some say that Heaven is Hell, some say that Hell is Heaven

I must admit, just when I think I'm King – I just begin
Just when I think I'm King, I must admit – I just begin
Just when I think I'm King
I just begin

I've been doing it for years, my goal is moving near
It says 'Look, I'm over here', then it up and disappear
Some say that knowledge is something sat in your lap
Some say that knowledge is oh-oh-oh-oh
I want to be a lawyer, I want to be a scholar
But I really can't be bothered, ooh just
Gimme it quick, gimme it, gimme, gimme, gimme, gimme

Some say that knowledge is oh-oh-oh
Some say that knowledge is oh-oh-oh
Some say that Heaven is Hell, some say that Hell is Heaven

I must admit just when I think I'm King – I just begin
Just when I think I'm King, I must admit – I just begin
Just when I think everything's going great – I just begin

I get the break
Hey I'm gonna take it all – I just begin
When I'm King
Just begin

In my dome of ivory, a home of activity
I want the answers quickly, but I don't have no energy
I hold a cup of wisdom, but there is nothing within
My cup she never overfloweth and 'tis I that moan and
    groaneth
It's a grey and white matter
Give me the Karma Mama
I'm coming up the ladder
Hey I'm coming up the ladder
A jet to Mecca
Up the ladder
Tibet or Jeddah
To Salisbury
A monastery
The longest journey
Across the desert
Across the weather
Across the elements
Across the water

Eye of Braille
Hem of Anorak
Stem of Wallflower
Hair of Doormat

Under the Ivy

It wouldn't take me long
To tell you how to find it
To tell you where we'll meet
This little girl inside me
Is retreating to her favourite place

Go into the garden
Go under the ivy
Under the leaves
Away from the party
Go right to the rose
Go right to the white rose for me

I sit here in the thunder
The green on the grey
I feel it all around me
And it's not easy for me
To give away a secret
It's not safe but

Go into the garden
Go under the ivy
Under the leaves
Away from the party
Go right to the rose
Go right to the white rose for me

Go into the garden
Go under the ivy
Go under the leaves with me

Go right to the rose
Go right to the white rose
I'll be waiting for you

It wouldn't take me long
To tell you how to find it

And So Is Love

And you, huh?
You do, huh?

We let it in
We give it out
And in the end
What's it all about?
It must be love

I give you my
I give you my
You give me your
You give me your joy

> We used to say
> 'Ah Hell, we're young'
> But now we see that life is sad
> And so is love

Ooh baby, live your life for love
Ooh baby, live your life for love

> We used to say
> 'Ah Hell, we're young'
> But now we see that life is sad
> And so is love

Ooh baby, for the sake of love
Ooh baby, for the sake of love

And whatever happens
What really matters?
It's all we've got
Isn't that enough?

Life is sad and so is love

You let it slip
You let it slip
I love you more
I love you more for it

Life is sad and so is love

All for love
Just for the sake of love
You set me free
I set you free

Running Up That Hill (A Deal with God)

It doesn't hurt me
Do you want to feel how it feels?
Do you want to know, know that it doesn't hurt me?
Do you want to hear about the deal that I'm making?

You
It's you and me

And if I only could
I'd make a deal with God
And I'd get him to swap our places
Be running up that road
Be running up that hill
Be running up that building
If I only could

You don't want to hurt me
But see how deep the bullet lies
Unaware I'm tearing you asunder
There is thunder in our hearts
Is there so much hate for the ones we love?
Tell me we both matter, don't we?

You
It's you and me
It's you and me won't be unhappy

If I only could
I'd make a deal with God
And I'd get him to swap our places

Be running up that road
Be running up that hill
Be running up that building
If I only could

You
It's you and me
It's you and me won't be unhappy

C'mon baby, c'mon darlin'
Let me steal this moment from you now
Come on angel, c'mon, c'mon darling
Let's exchange the experience

If I only could
I'd make a deal with God
And I'd get him to swap our places
I'd be running up that road
Be running up that hill
With no problem

Say if I only could
I'd be running up that hill
With no problem.

Snowed In at Wheeler Street

Excuse me, I'm sorry to bother you
but don't I know you?
There's just something about you
Haven't we met before?

'We've been in love forever'

When we got to the top of the hill
we saw Rome burning
I just let you walk away.
I've never forgiven myself

'I saw you on the steps in Paris,
you were with someone else
Couldn't you see that should've been me?
I just walked on by'

Then we met in 'forty-two
But we were on different sides
I hid you under my bed
But they took you away

'I lost you in a London smog
As you crossed the lane
I never know where you're gonna be next
but I know that you'll surprise me'

Come with me, I'll find some rope
and I'll tie us together
I've been waiting for you so long

I don't want to lose you again
Don't walk into the crowd again
Don't walk away again

I don't want to lose you
I don't want to lose you
I don't want to lose you again

'There's just something about you
Have we been in love forever?'

9/11 in New York, I took your photograph
I still have your smiling face . . .
In a heart-shaped frame

'Snowed in at Wheeler Street
Just two old flames
Keeping the fire going
We look so good together'

Can't we just stay there forever?
We were so happy
I'd live that day over and over
But the world won't stop turning

'When we got to the top of the hill
We saw Rome burning
I don't want to lose you,
I don't want to lose you again'

Don't walk away again
Don't leave me lost again

I don't want to lose you
I don't want to lose you
I don't want to lose you again
I don't want to lose you
I don't want to lose you
I don't want to lose you again
Oh no, not again!
Not again!
Oh no, no not again!
Not again!
Not again!
Never again!

Between a Man and a Woman

With her hand in his hand
They were both happy again
You started taking sides
They started arguing
He said it was her fault
She said it wasn't at all
But the truth lies somewhere in the middle

Where angels fear to tread you go rushing in
Well I had to tell you then
And now I'm telling you again
Stay out of this
You must not interfere
Don't you see this is
Between a man and a woman?

Every day and night, I pray
Pray that you will stay away forever
It's so hard for love to stay together
With the modern Western pressures
I don't want to say it
But I had to tell you then
And now I'm telling you again

Stay out of this
Oh, I know you mean to help me
And I know you've good intentions
But stay out of this
This isn't your problem
Do not interfere – you are not needed here

Let the pendulum swing
Between a man and a woman

Don't you see you're in the way?
Between a man and a woman
Every day and night I pray

Let the pendulum swing
Between a man and a woman

You're the One

It's alright I'll come 'round when
You're not in
And I'll pick up all my things
Everything I have, I bought with you
But that's alright too
It's just everything I do
We did together
And there's a little piece of you
In whatever

I've got everything I need
I've got petrol in the car
I've got some money with me
There's just one problem

You're the only one I want
You're the only one I want
You're the only one I want
You're the only one I want

It's alright I know where I'm going
I'm going to stay with my friend
Mmm, yes, he is very good looking
The only trouble is
He's not you
He can't do what you do
He can't make me laugh and cry
At the same time

Let's change things
Let's danger it up
We're crazy enough
I just can't take it

You're the only one I want
You're the only one I want
You're the only one I want
You're the only one I want

I know where I'm going
But I don't want to leave
I just have one problem

We're best friends, yeah?

We tied ourselves in knots
Doing cartwheels 'cross the floor
Just forget it alright
Sugar? . . .
Honey? . . .
Sugar? . . .
Trouble

All the Love

The first time I died
Was in the arms of good friends of mine
They kiss me with tears
They hadn't been near me for years
Say why do it now
When I won't be around, I'm going out?

'We needed you to love us too. We wait for your move'

Only tragedy allows the release
Of love and grief never normally seen
I didn't want to let them see me weep
I didn't want to let them see me weak
But I know I have shown
That I stand at the gates alone

'We needed you to love us too. We wait for your move'

All the love, all the love, all the love you should have given
All the love, all the love, all the love we could have given
All the love, all the love, all the love

The next time, I dedicate
My life's work to the friends I make
I give them what they want to hear
They think I'm up to something weird
And up rears the head of fear in me

So now when they ring
I get my machine to let them in

'We needed you to love us too. We wait for your move'

All the love, all the love, all the love you should have given
All the love, all the love, all the love we could have given
All the love, all the love, all the love

'Take care, toodle-ooh'
'Bye bye'
'Bye for now, love'
'Bye'
'Later'
'Bye-ee'
'Cheerio'
'Bye'
'Bye bye'
'Bye'
'See ya'
'Bye-ee'
'Bye'
'Bye'
'Cheers'
'See ya, love'
'Bye'
'Goodbye'
'I'll see ya soon'
'Goodnight'

'We needed you to love us too. We wait for your move'

I found a book on how to be invisible
On the edge of the Labyrinth
Under a veil you must never lift

Army Dreamers

Our little Army Boy
Is coming home from B.F.P.O.
I've a bunch of purple flowers
To decorate a mammy's hero
Mourning in the aerodrome
The weather warmer, he is colder
Four men in uniform to carry home
My little soldier

'What could he do?
Should have been a rock star'
But he didn't have the money for a guitar
'What could he do?
Should have been a politician'
But he never had a proper education
'What could he do?
Should have been a father'
But he never even made it to his twenties
What a waste
Army Dreamers

Tears o'er a tin box
Oh Jesus Christ, he wasn't to know
Like a chicken with a fox
He couldn't win the war with ego
Give the kid the pick of pips
And give him all your stripes and ribbons
Now he's sitting in his hole
He might as well have buttons and bows

What could he do?
Should have been a rock star
But he didn't have the money for a guitar
What could he do?
Should have been a politician
But he never had a proper education
What could he do?
Should have been a father
But he never even made it to his twenties
What a waste
Army Dreamers

Pull Out the Pin

Just as we hit the green
I've never been so happy to be alive
Only seven miles behind
You could smell the child
The smell of the front line's survival
With my silver Buddha
And my silver bullet
I pull the pin

You learn to ride the Earth
When you're living on your belly
And the enemy is city birth
Who need radar?
We use scent
They stink of the west,
Stink of sweat
Stink of cologne and baccy
And their Yankee Hash
With my silver Buddha
And my silver bullet
Pulling on the pin
Pull out, pull out the pin
Pulling on the pin

Just one thing in it, me or him
And I love life
Pull out the pin
Just one thing in it, me or him
And I love life
Pull out the pin

Just one thing in it, me or him
And I love life, I love life, I love life
Pull out the pin

I've seen the coat for me
I'll track him 'til he drops
Then I'll pop him one he won't see
He's big and pink and not like me
He sees no light
He sees no reason for the fighting
With my silver Buddha
And my silver bullet
I pull the pin

I had not seen his face
'Til I'm only feet away
Unbeknown to my prey
I look in American eyes
I see little life
See little wife

He's striking violence up in me
With my silver Buddha
And my silver bullet
Pulling on the pin
Pull out, pull out the pin
Pulling on the pin

Just one thing in it, me or him
And I love life

Pull out the pin
Just one thing in it, me or him
And I love life
Pull out the pin
Just one thing in it, me or him
And I love life, I love life, I love life
Pull out the pin

Just one thing in it, me or him
And I love life
So I pull out the pin
Just one thing in it, me or him
And I love life
So I pull out the pin
Just one thing in it, me or him and I love life,
I love life, I love life, I love life, I love life . . .
Pull out the pin

Breathing

Outside gets inside
Through her skin
I've been out before
But this time it's much safer in
Last night, in the sky
Such a bright light
My radar send me danger
But my instincts tell me to
Keep Breathing

Breathing
Breathing my mother in
Breathing my beloved in
Breathing, Breathing her nicotine, breathing
Breathing the fall out-in, out-in, out-in, out-in, out-in

We've lost our chance
We're the first and last
After the blast
Chips of Plutonium are twinkling in every lung
I love my beloved
All and everywhere
Only the fools blew it
You and me knew life itself is breathing

Breathing
Breathing my mother in
Breathing my beloved in
Breathing, Breathing her nicotine, breathing
Breathing the fall out-in, out-in, out-in, out-in, out-in

What are we going to do without?
Oh, please
Let me breathe
Quick – breathe in deep
We are all going to die without
Leave me something to breathe
Oh God, please leave us something to breathe
What are we going to do without?
Life is –
Breathing

Experiment IV

We were working secretly for the military
Our experiment in sound was nearly ready to begin
We only know in theory what we are doing
Music made for pleasure, music made to thrill
It was music we were making here until

They told us all they wanted
Was a sound that could kill someone from a distance
So we go ahead and the meters are over in the red
It's a mistake in the making

From the painful cries of mothers to a terrifying scream
We recorded it and put it into our machine

They told us all they wanted
Was a sound that could kill someone from a distance
So we go ahead and the meters are over in the red
It's a mistake in the making

It could feel like falling in love
It could feel so bad
It could feel so good
It could sing you to sleep
But that dream is your enemy

We won't be there to be blamed
We won't be there to snitch
I just pray that someone there can hit the switch

They told us all they wanted
Was a sound that could kill someone from a distance
So we go ahead and the meters are over in the red
It's a mistake we have made

And the public are warned to stay off

Joanni

All the banners stop waving
And the flags stop flying
And the silence comes over
Thousands of soldiers
Thousands of soldiers

Who is that girl? Do I know her face?
Who is that girl?

Joanni, Joanni wears a golden cross
And she looks so beautiful in her armour
Joanni, Joanni blows a kiss to God
And she never wears a ring on her finger

All the cannon are firing
And the swords are clashing
And the horses are charging
And the flags are flying
And the battle is raging
And the bells, the bells are ringing

Who is that girl? Do I know her face?
Who is that girl?

Joanni, Joanni wears a golden cross
And she looks so beautiful in her armour
Joanni, Joanni blows a kiss to God
And she never wears a ring on her finger
Joanni, Joanni, Joanni, Joanni blows a kiss to God

And she just looks beautiful in her armour
Beautiful in her armour

Elle parle à Dieu et aux anges
Dans ses prières

Venez Sainte Catherine
Venez Sainte Marguerite
Elle a besoin de vous deux
Les voix, les voix du feu
Chantent avec ma petite soeur
Les voix, les voix, les voix

England My Lionheart

Oh England, my Lionheart,
I'm in your garden, fading fast in your arms
The soldiers soften, the war is over
The air raid shelters are blooming clover
Flapping umbrellas fill the lanes
My London Bridge in rain again

Oh England, my Lionheart,
Peter Pan steals the kids in Kensington Park
You read me Shakespeare on the rolling Thames
That old river poet that never, ever ends
Our thumping hearts hold the ravens in
And keep the tower from tumbling

Oh England, my Lionheart
Oh England, my Lionheart
Oh England, my Lionheart
I don't want to go

Oh England, my Lionheart,
Dropped from my black Spitfire to my funeral barge
Give me one kiss in apple-blossom
Give me one wish, and I'd be wassailing
In the orchard, my English rose
Or with my shepherd who'll bring me home

Oh England, my Lionheart
Oh England, my Lionheart
Oh England, my Lionheart
I don't want to go

Oh England, my Lionheart
Oh England, my Lionheart
Oh England, my Lionheart
I don't want to go

Pages you must never turn
In the Labyrinth ...

A Coral Room

There's a city, draped in net
Fisherman net
And in the half-light, in the half-light
It looks like every tower
Is covered in webs
Moving and glistening and rocking
Its babies in rhythm
As the spider of time is climbing
Over the ruins

There were hundreds of people living here
Sails at the windows
And the 'planes came crashing down
And many a pilot drowned
And the speed boats flying above
Put your hand over the side of the boat
What do you feel?

My mother and her little brown jug
It held her milk
And now it holds our memories
I can hear her singing
'Little brown jug, don't I love thee?'
'Little brown jug, don't I love thee?'
Ho ho ho, hee hee hee

I hear her laughing
She is standing in the kitchen
As we come in the back door
See it fall

See it fall
Oh little spider climbing out of a broken jug
And the pieces will lay there a while
In a house draped in net
In a room filled with coral
Sails at the window
Forests of masts
Put your hand over the side of the boat
Put your hand over the side of the boat
What do you feel?

Deeper Understanding

As the people here grow colder
I turn to my computer
And spend my evenings with it
Like a friend
I was loading a new program
I had ordered from a magazine
'Are you lonely, are you lost?
This voice console is a must'
I press Execute

'Hello, I know that you've been feeling tired
I bring you love and deeper understanding
Hello, I know that you're unhappy
I bring you love and deeper understanding'

Well I've never felt such pleasure
Nothing else seemed to matter
I neglected my bodily needs
I did not eat, I did not sleep
The intensity increasing
'Til my family found me and intervened
But I was lonely, I was lost
Without my little black box
I pick up the 'phone and go Execute

'Hello, I know that you've been feeling tired
I bring you love and deeper understanding
Hello, I know that you're unhappy
I bring you love and deeper understanding'

I turn to my computer like a friend
Hallo? Hallo?
I need deeper understanding
Give me deeper understanding

I hate to leave you
I hate to leave you
I hate to lose you

The Infant Kiss

I say Goodnight night
I tuck him in tight
But things are not right
What is this?
An infant kiss
That sends my body tingling
I've never fallen for
A little boy before
     No control
Just a kid and just at school
Back home they'd call me dirty
His little hand is on my heart
He's got me where it hurts me
Knock, knock, who's there in this baby?
You know how to work me

All my barriers are going
It's starting to show
Let's go, let's go
Let go, let go
Let go

I cannot sit and let
Something happen I'll regret
Ooh, he scares me
There's a man behind those eyes
I catch him
When I'm bending
Ooh, how he frightens me
When they whisper privately

Windy wailey blows me
Words of caress on their lips
That speak of adult love
I want to smack
But I hold back
I only want to touch
I must stay and find a way
To stop before it gets too much

All my barriers are going
It's starting to show
Let's go, let's go
Let go, let go
Let go

Misty

Roll his body
Give him eyes
Make him smile for me
Give him life
My hand is bleeding, I run back inside

I turn off the light
Switch on a starry night
My window flies open
My bedroom fills with falling snow
Should be a dream but I'm not sleepy
I see his snowy white face but I'm not afraid
He lies down beside me
So cold next to me
I can feel him melting in my hand
Melting, in my hand

He won't speak to me
His crooked mouth is full of dead leaves
Full of dead leaves, bits of twisted branches
And frozen garden
Crushed and stolen grasses
From slumbering lawn
He is dissolving, dissolving before me
And dawn will come soon
What kind of spirit is this?
Our one and only tryst
His breath all misty
And when I kiss his ice-cream lips
And his creamy skin

His snowy white arms surround me
So cold next to me
I can feel him melting in my hand
Melting, melting, in my hand

Sunday morning
I can't find him
The sheets are soaking
And on my pillow:

Dead leaves, bits of twisted branches
And frozen garden
Crushed and stolen grasses
From slumbering lawn
I can't find him – Misty . . .
Oh please can you help me?
He must be somewhere
Open window closing
Oh but wait, it's still snowing
If you're out there
I'm coming out on the ledge
I'm going out on the ledge

The Red Shoes

Oh she move like the Diva do
I said, 'I'd love to dance like you.'
She said, 'Just take off my red shoes
Put them on and your
Dream'll come true
With no words, with no song
You can dance the dream
With your body on
And this curve, is your smile
And this cross, is your heart
And this line, is your path

Oh it's gonna be the way you always
Thought it would be
But it's gonna be no illusion
Oh it's gonna be the way you always dreamt about it
But it's gonna be really happening to ya
Really happening to ya
Really happening to ya'

Oh the minute I put them on
I knew I had done something wrong
All her gifts for the dance had gone
It's the red shoes, they can't
Stop dancing, dancing
And this curve, is your smile
And this cross, is your heart
And this line, is your path

'Oh it's gonna be the way you always
Thought it would be
But it's gonna be no illusion
Oh it's gonna be the way you always dreamt about it
But it's gonna be really happening to ya

'She gotta dance, she gotta dance
And she can't stop 'til them shoes come off
These shoes do, a kind of voodoo
They're gonna make her dance
'Til her legs fall off'

Feel your hair come tumbling down
Feel your feet start kissing the ground
Feel your arms are opening out
And see your eyes are lifted to God
With no words, with no song
I'm gonna dance the dream
And make the dream come true
I'm gonna dance the dream
And make the dream come true

'She gotta dance, she gotta dance
And she can't stop 'til them shoes come off
These shoes do, a kind of voodoo
They're gonna make her dance
'Til her legs fall off
Call a doctor, call a priest
They're gonna whip her up like
A helicopter'

Really happening to ya
Really happening to ya

You gotta dance . . .

Lily

Well I said:
'Lily, Oh Lily I don't feel safe
I feel like life has blown a great big hole through me'
And she said:
'Child, you must protect yourself
You must protect yourself
I'll show you how with fire'

Gabriel before me
Raphael behind me
Michael to my right
Uriel on my left side
In the circle of fire

I said:
'Lily, Oh Lily I'm so afraid
I fear I am walking in the Vale of Darkness'
And she said:
'Child, take what I say
With a pinch of salt
And protect yourself with fire'

Gabriel before me
Raphael behind me
Michael to my right
Uriel on my left side
In the circle of fire

Among Angels

Only you can do something about it
There's no-one there, my friend, any better
I might know what you mean when you say you fall apart
Aren't we all the same – in and out of doubt?

I can see angels standing around you
They shimmer like mirrors in Summer
But you don't know it

And they will carry you o'er the walls
If you need us, just call
Rest your weary world in their hands
Lay your broken laugh at their feet

I can see angels around you
They shimmer like mirrors in Summer
There's someone who's loved you forever
But you don't know it
You might feel it and just not show it

The Fog

You see, I'm all grown up now
He said:
'Just put your feet down child
'Cause you're all grown-up now'
Just like a photograph I pick you up
Just like a station on the radio I pick you up
Just like a face in the crowd
I pick you up
Just like a feeling that you're sending out
I pick it up
But I can't let you go
If I let you go
You slip into the fog . . .

This love was big enough for the both of us,
This love of yours,
Was big enough to be frightened of
It's deep and dark like the water was
The day I learned to swim

He said:
'Just put your feet down, child
The water is only waist-high
I'll let go of you gently
Then you can swim to me'

Is this love big enough to watch over me
Big enough to let go of me
Without hurting me
Like the day I learned to swim?

'Cause you're all grown-up now
Just put your feet down, child
The water is only waist-high
I'll let go of you gently
Then you can swim to me'

You stand in front of
a million doors
And each one holds
a million more
Corridors that lead to the World
Of the Invisible

A SKY OF HONEY

Prelude

Mummy . . .
Daddy . . .
The day is full of birds
Sounds like they're saying words

Prologue

We're gonna be laughing about this
We're gonna be dancing around
It's gonna be so good now
It's gonna be so good

Oh so exciting, mmh go on and on
Every time you leave us
So Summer will be gone
So you'll never grow old to us

It's gonna be so good now
It's gonna be so good
Can you see the lark ascending?

Oh so romantic, swept me off my feet
Like some kind of magic
Like the light in Italy
Lost its way across the sea . . .

Roma, Roma mia
Tesora mia, bella
Piena di sole luce
Bali così bene, bene
Pianissimo
Pianissimo

What a lovely afternoon
What a lovely afternoon
Oh can you hear the birdsong:
The mistle thrush and wood pigeon

The chaffinch and the robin
The blackbird and the siskin
Like golden light dripping and golden bells?
Ding dong, ding dong
Ding dong, ding dong
Ring it, shake it down, bring it on, let it in
Ring it, shake it down, bring it on, let it in
Summer has come
Summer be long
What a lovely afternoon
What a lovely afternoon
Oh will you come with us to find
The song of the oil and the brush?

An Architect's Dream

Watching the painter painting
And all the time, the light is changing
And he keeps painting
That bit there, it was an accident
But he's so pleased
It's the best mistake he could make
And it's my favourite piece
It's just great

The flick of a wrist
Twisting down to the hips
So the lovers begin, with a kiss
In a tryst
It's just a smudge
But what it becomes
In his hands:
Curving and sweeping
Rising and reaching
I could feel what he was feeling
Lines like these have got to be
An architect's dream

It's always the same
Whenever he works on a pavement
It starts to rain
And all the time
The light is changing

The Painter's Link

It's raining
What has become of my painting?
All the colours are running

So all the colours run
So all the colours run
See what they have become –
A wonderful sunset

Sunset

Could be honeycomb
In a sea of honey
A sky of honey
Whose shadow, long and low
Is slipping out of wet clothes?
And changes into
The most beautiful
Iridescent blue

Who knows who wrote that song of Summer
That blackbirds sing at dusk?
This is a song of colour
Where sands sing in crimson, red and rust
Then climb into bed and turn to dust

Every sleepy light
Must say goodbye
To the day before it dies
In a sea of honey
A sky of honey
Keep us close to your hearts
So if the skies turn dark
We may live on in
Comets and stars

Who knows who wrote that song of Summer
That blackbirds sing at dusk?
This is a song of colour
Where sands sing in crimson, red and rust
Then climb into bed and turn to dust

Who knows who wrote that song of Summer
That blackbirds sing at dusk?
This is a song of colour
Where sands sing in crimson, red and rust
Then climb into bed and turn to dust

Oh sing of Summer and a sunset
And sing for us, so that we may remember
The day writes the words right across the sky
They go all the way up to the top of the night

Aerial Tal
(A brief text on how to speak blackbird)

Somewhere in Between

We went up to the top of the highest hill and stopped
Still

It was just so beautiful
It was just so beautiful
It was just so beautiful

This is where the shadows come to play
'Twixt the day
And night
Dancing and skipping
Along a chink of light

Somewhere in between
The waxing and the waning wave
Somewhere in between
What the song and silence says
Somewhere in between
The ticking and the tocking clock
Somewhere in a dream between
Sleep and waking up
Somewhere in between
Breathing out and breathing in
Like twilight is neither night nor morning

Not one of us would dare to break
The silence
Oh how we have longed
For something that would
Make us feel so

Somewhere in between
The waxing and the waning wave
Somewhere in between
The night and the daylight
Somewhere in between
The ticking and the tocking clock
Somewhere in between
What the song and the silence say

Somewhere in between
Breathing out and breathing in

It was a lovely afternoon
Such a lovely afternoon
Sinking down into the hills
The pillows in the hills
Tesoro mio
Gioiello mio
Il sole
Il cielo

Goodnight, sun
Goodnight, sun

Goodnight, Mum

Tawny Moon

I'll give every cloud a silver lining
Every star will be bright and shining
Tawny owls swoop, the howling wolf
Every swimming pool will shiver with excitement
I've made the wind blow and starry heavens hang
I ache from head to toe, I've got blisters on my hands

Oh man, I'm painting the moon tonight
Oh man, I'm painting the moon tonight

She's been travelling o'er the plains of Africa
Climbing every mountain near and far
Near and far, far and near
Oh my love, my love, my Luna is nearly here
Here comes the night, she shimmies across the strand
I've got to get it just right, I've got blisters on my hands

Ladies and gentlemen
We present to you tonight . . . the Moon!
Come on, don't be shy!

Tawny Moon
I'm gonna dance all night with the Tawny Moon

Just a touch of glimmer mixed with the glow
I will paint the face that has made the oceans roll
Ripe and full, mystical
Oh my love, my love, my Luna I hear you call
She wrote the book on love then threw it away
You'd better all behave when Luna takes the stage

Oh man, look at the moon tonight
Oh man, a magical moon tonight

Can you hear the nightingale sweetly sigh?
She knows precisely why the unrequited poet cries
She comes, she goes, she goes, she comes

Oh my love, my love, my Luna Queen of Bedlam
Make the woodwind blow and strike up the band
I've got to get it just right, I've got blisters on my hands

Rise and shine, Tawny Moon
I'm gonna paint all night with the Tawny Moon
I'm gonna dance all night with the Tawny Moon

Nocturn

Sweet dreams . . .

On this Midsummer night
Everyone is sleeping
We go driving into the moonlight

Could be in a dream
Our clothes are on the beach
These prints of our feet
Lead right up to the sea
No-one, no-one is here
No-one, no-one is here
We stand in the Atlantic
We become panoramic

We tire of the city
We tire of it all
We long for just that something more

Could be in a dream
Our clothes are on the beach
The prints of our feet
Lead right up to the sea
No-one, no-one is here
No-one, no-one is here
We stand in the Atlantic
We become panoramic

The stars are caught in our hair
The stars are on our fingers

A veil of diamond dust
Just reach up and touch it
The sky's above our heads
The sea's around our legs
In milky, silky water
We swim further and further

We dive down . . . We dive down

A diamond night, a diamond sea
and a diamond sky . . .

We dive deeper and deeper
we dive deeper and deeper
Could be we are here
Could be in a dream

It came up on the horizon
Rising and rising
In a sea of honey, a sky of honey
A sea of honey, a sky of honey

Look at the light, all the time it's a-changing
Look at the light, climbing up the aerial
Bright, white coming alive jumping off of the aerial
All the time it's a-changing, like now . . .
All the time it's a-changing, like then again . . .
All the time it's a-changing
And all the dreamers are waking

Aerial

The dawn has come
And the wine will run
And the song must be sung
And the flowers are melting
In the sun

I feel I want to be up on the roof
I feel I gotta get up on the roof
Up, up on the roof
Up, up on the roof

Oh the dawn has come
And the song must be sung
And the flowers are melting
What kind of language is this?

What kind of language is this?
I can't hear a word you're saying
Tell me what are you singing?
In the sun

All of the birds are laughing
All of the birds are laughing
Come on, let's all join in
Come on, let's all join in

Look at my beautiful wings!
My beautiful wings

I want to be up on the roof
I've gotta be up on the roof
Up, up high on the roof
Up, up on the roof
In the sun

Corridors that twist and turn
Corridors that blister and burn

Houdini

I wait at the table and hold hands with weeping strangers
Wait for you to join the group
The tambourine jingle-jangles
The medium
    Roams and rambles
Not taken in,
    I break the circle
I want this man to go away now

With a kiss, I'd pass the key
And feel your tongue
Teasing and receiving

With your spit still on my lip
You hit the water

Him and I in the room
To prove you are with us too
He's using code that only you and I know
This is no trick of his
This is your magic
I'd catch the queues watching you
Hoping you'd do something wrong
Everybody thinks you'll never make it
But every time, you escape
Rosabel, believe, not even Eternity
Can hold Houdini
    Rosabel, believe

Through the glass, I'd watch you breathe

Bound and drowned
And paler than you've ever been

With your life the only thing in my mind
We pull you from the water

Houdini

You and I and Rosabel believe

Heads We're Dancing

You talked me into the game of chance
It was 'thirty-nine before the music started
When you walked up to me and you said
'Hey, heads we dance'
Well, I didn't know who you were
Until I saw the morning paper

There was a picture of you
A picture of you 'cross the front page
It looked just like you, just like you in every way
But it couldn't be true
It couldn't be true
You stepped out of a stranger

They say that the Devil is a charming man
And just like you I bet he can dance
And he's coming up behind in his
Long-tailed black coat dance
All tails in the air
But the penny landed with its head dancing

A picture of you, a picture of you in uniform
Standing with your head held high
Hot down to the floor
But it couldn't be you
It couldn't be you
It's a picture of Hitler

He go do-do-do-do-do
He go do-do-do-do-do

He go do-do-do-do-do
Do you want to dance?
Well, I couldn't see what was to be
So I just stood there laughing

A picture of you, a picture of you in uniform
Standing with your head held high
Hot down to the floor
But it couldn't be you
It couldn't be you
It's a picture of Hitler

He go mmh-mmh-mmh-mmh-mmh
He go mmh-mmh-mmh-mmh-mmh
He go mmh-mmh-mmh-mmh-mmh
Heads we're dancing

Walk Straight Down the Middle

Can't move my arms
Can't move my legs
Can't say no
I can't say yes
Can't help myself
I need your help

Ooh, what do we do?
We just can't move
We're calling out for Middle Street

Ooh, what do we do?
Now we just can't move
We hang on to every line
And walk straight down the middle of it

He thought he was gonna die
But he didn't
She thought she just couldn't cope
But she did
We thought it would be so hard
But it wasn't
It wasn't easy, though

I can't say yes
I can't say no
Can't begin
Can't let go
Help me now

Ooh, what do we do?
Now we just can't move
We're calling out for Middle Street

Ooh, ooh, what do we do?
Now we just can't move
We hang on to every line
And walk straight down the middle of it

He thought he was gonna die
But he didn't
She thought she could never cope
But she did
And we thought it was all over
But it wasn't
It hadn't started yet
No, no

Who just got fooled?
And walk straight down the middle of it
And walk straight down the middle of it

Calling out for Middle Street
Calling out for Middle Street

Walking straight down the middle of it

The Dreaming

BANG goes another kanga
On the bonnet of the van

See the light ram through the gaps in the land

Many an Aborigine's mistaken for a tree
'Til you near him on the motorway
The tree begin to breathe

See the light ram through the gaps in the land

Coming in with the golden light – in the morning
Coming in with the golden light – is the New Man
Coming in with the golden light – is my dented van
Woomera

DRE-A-M-T-I-ME

The civilised keep alive the territorial war

See the light ram through the gaps in the land

Erase the race that claim the place
And say we dig for ore
Or dangle Devils in a bottle
And push them from the pull of the bush

See the light ram through the gaps in the land

You find them in the road

See the light bounce off the rocks to the sand

In the road

Coming in with the golden light – in the morning
Coming in with the golden light – with no warning
Coming in with the golden light – we bring in the rigging
Dig, dig, dig, dig away

DRE-A-M-T-I-ME

M-M-Many an Aborigine's mistaken for a tree

See the light ram through the gaps in the land

You near him on the motorway, the tree begin to breathe
Erase the race that claim the place and say we dig for ore

See the light ram through the gaps in the land

Dangle Devils in a bottle
And push them from the pull of the bush

See the sun set in the hand of the man

BANG goes another kanga
On the bonnet of the van

See the light bounce off the rocks to the sand

You find them in the road

See the light ram through the gaps in the land

In the road

See the light

Push 'em from the pull of the bush

See the light bounce off the rocks to the sand

Push 'em from the pull of the bush

See the sun set in the hand of the man

Wild Man

They call you an animal, the Kangchenjunga Demon, Wild
  Man, Metoh-Kangmi
Lying in my tent, I can hear your cry echoing round the
  mountainside
You sound lonely
While crossing the Lhakpa-La something jumped down from
  the rocks
In the remote Garo Hills by Dipu Marak we found footprints
  in the snow

The schoolmaster of Darjeeling said he saw you by the
  Tengboche Monastery
You were playing in the snow. You were banging on the doors.
  You got up on the roof
Roof of the World
You were pulling up the rhodedendrons. Loping down the
  mountain
They want to know you. They will hunt you down, then they
  will kill you
Run away, run away, run away . . .
While crossing the Lhakpa-La something jumped down from
  the rocks
In the remote Garo Hills by Dipu Marak we found footprints
  in the snow
We found your footprints in the snow. We brushed them all
  away . . .
From the Sherpas of Annapurna to the Rinpoche of Qinghai
Shepherds from Mount Kailash to Himachal Pradesh found
  footprints in the snow

You're not a langur monkey nor a big brown bear – you're the
    Wild Man
They say they saw you drowned near the Rongbuk Glacier
They want to hunt you down. You're not an animal
The Lamas say you're not an animal

Moving

Moving stranger, does it really matter?
As long as you're not afraid to feel
Touch me, hold me, how my open arms ache
Try to fall for me

How I'm moved, how you move me
With your beauty's potency
You give me life, please don't let me go
You crush the lily in my soul

Moving liquid, yes, you are just as water
You flow around all that comes in your way
Don't think it over, it always takes you over
And sets your spirit dancing

How I'm moved, how you move me
With your beauty's potency
You give me life, please don't let me go
You crush the lily in my soul

Rubberband Girl

See those trees
Bend in the wind
I feel they've got a lot more
Sense than me
You see I try to resist

A rubberband bouncing back to life
A rubberband bend the beat
If I could learn to give like
A rubberband
I'd be back on my feet
A rubberband hold me trousers up
A rubberband ponytails
If I could learn to twang like
A rubberband
I'd be a rubberband girl
A rubberband girl me
A rubberband girl me
Oh I wanna be a rubberband girl

When I slip out
Of my catapult
I gotta land with my feet firm
On the ground
And let my body catch up

A rubberband bouncing back to life
A rubberband bend the beat
If I could learn to give like
A rubberband

I'd be back on my feet
A rubberband hold me trousers up
A rubberband ponytails
If I could learn to twang like
A rubberband
I'd be a rubberband girl
A rubberband girl me
A rubberband girl me
Oh I wanna be a rubberband girl

Give like a rubberband
Twang like a rubberband
Snap like a rubberband

Rub-a-dub-a-dub-a-dub
Rub-a-dub-a-dub
Rub-a-dub

One rubberband won't keep you up
Two rubberbands won't keep you up
Three rubberbands won't keep you up

Here I go . . .
. . . Yeah!

One rubberband won't keep you up
Two rubberbands won't keep you up
Three rubberbands won't keep you up

There Goes a Tenner

Okay remember, okay remember
That we have just allowed
Half an hour,
To get in, do it and get out
The sense of adventure
Is changing to danger
The signal has been given
I go in
The crime begins

My excitement
Turns into fright
All my words fade
What am I gonna say?
Mustn't give the game away

We're waiting

We got the job sussed,
This shop's shut for business
The look-out has parked the car,
But kept the engine running
Three beeps means trouble's coming
I hope you remember
To treat the gelignite tenderly for me
I'm having dreams about things
Not going right
Let's leave in plenty of time tonight

Both my partners
Act like actors
You are Bogart
He is George Raft
That leaves Cagney and me

We're waiting

You blow the safe up
Then all I know is I wake up
Covered in rubble
One of the rabble
Needs mummy
The government will never find the money
I've been here all day
A star in strange ways
Apart from a photograph
They'll get nothing from me
Not until they let me see
My solicitor
Ooh I remember
That rich windy weather
When you would carry me
Pockets floating in the breeze
There goes a tenner
Hey look, there's a fiver
There's a ten shilling note
Remember them?
That's when we used to vote for him

Suspended in Gaffa

Out in the garden, there's half of a Heaven
And we're only bluffing
We're not ones for busting through walls
But they've told us unless we can prove
That we're doing it
We can't have it all

And I want it all

He's gonna wangle a way to get out of it
She's an excuse
And a witness who'll talk when he's called,
But they've told us unless we can prove
That we're doing it
We can't have it all

And I want it all
And I want it all
We can't have it all
And I want it all
I caught a glimpse of a god
All shining and bright

Suddenly my feet are feet of mud
It all goes slo-mo
I don't know why I'm crying
Am I suspended in Gaffa?
Not until I'm ready for you
Not until I'm ready for you
Can I have it all

I try to get nearer
But as it gets clearer
There's something appears in the way
It's a plank in me eye
With a camel who's trying to get through it
Am I doing it?
Can I have it all now?
And I want it all

I pull out the plank
And say thank ye for yanking me back
To the fact
That there's always something to distract
But sometimes it's hard
To know if I'm doing it right
Can I have it all now?

And I want it all
Can I have it all now?
And I want it all
Can I have it all?
And I want it all
I can't have it all
We all have a dream
Maybe?

Suddenly my feet are feet of mud
It all goes slo-mo
I don't know why I'm crying
Am I suspended in Gaffa?

Not until I'm ready for you
Not until I'm ready for you
Can I have it all

I won't open boxes that I am told not to
I'm not a Pandora
I'm much more like
That girl in the mirror
Between you and me
She don't stand a chance of
Getting anywhere at all

And I want it all
Not anywhere at all
And I want it all
No, not a thing
And I want it all
She can't have it all
Mother, where are the angels?
I'm scared of the changes

Suddenly my feet are feet of mud
It all goes slo-mo
I don't know why I'm crying
Am I suspended in Gaffa?
Not until I'm ready for you
Not until I'm ready for you
Can I have it all

Leave It Open

With my ego in my gut
My babbling mouth would wash it up
    But now I've started learning how
        I keep it shut

My door was never locked
Until one day a trigger come cocking
    But now I've started learning how
        I keep it shut

Wide eyes would clean and dust
Things that decay, things that rust
    But now I've started learning how
        I keep them shut
        I keep them shut

        Harm is in us,
        Harm in us but power to arm
        Harm is in us,
        Harm in us but power to arm
        Harm is in us,
        Leave it open
        Harm in us but power to arm

Narrow mind would persecute it
Die a little to get to it
    But now I've started learning how
        I leave it open

I kept it in a cage
Watched it weeping, but I made it stay
   But now I've started learning how
        I leave it open
        I leave it open

        Harm is in us,
        Harm in us but power to arm
        Harm is in us
        Harm in us but power to arm
        Harm is in us
        Leave it open
        Harm in us but power to arm

        Harm is in us
        Harm in you and me
        What you letting in?
        Tell me what you're letting in
        Say what we're gonna let in:

We let the weirdness in

We let the weirdness in

We let the WEIRDNESS in

We let the WEIRDNESS in

We let the WEIRDNESS in

Big Stripey Lie

Oh big stripey lie moving
Like a wavy line
Coming up behind

All young gentle dreams drowning
In life's grief
Can you hang on me?

Don't want to hurt you, baby
I only want to help you
I could be good for you

Your name is being called by
Sacred things
That are not addressed nor listened to
Sometimes they blow trumpets

Only want to help you
Never want to hurt you
I know I could be good for you

Oh my God it's a jungle in here
You've got wild animals loose in here

Want to help you
Never hurt you
Good for you
Hey all you little waves run away
Mmm run away

Get Out of My House

When you left the door was slamming
You paused in the doorway
As though a thought stole you away
I watch the world pull you away
So I run into the hall
(Lock it)
Into the corridor
(Lock it)
There's a door in the house slamming
I hear the lift descending
I hear it hit the landing
See the hackles on the cat, standing
With my key I lock it
With my key I lock it up
With my key I lock it
With my key I lock it up

I am the concierge, chez-moi, honey
Won't letcha in for love nor money
My home, my joy
I'm barred and bolted and I
Won't letcha in

Get out of my house

No stranger's feet
Will enter me
I wash the panes
I clean the stains away

This house is as old as I am
This house knows all I have done
They come with their weather hanging around them
But can't knock my door down
With my key I lock it
With my key I lock it
This house is full of m-m-my mess
This house is full of m-m-mistakes
This house is full of m-m-madness
This house is full of, full of, full of fight
With my keeper I clean up
With my keeper I clean it all up
With my keeper I clean up
With my keeper I clean it all up

I am the concierge, chez-moi, honey
Won't letcha in for love nor money
My home, my joy I'm barred and bolted and I
Won't letcha in

Get out of my house

No stranger's feet
Will enter me
I wash the panes
I clean the stains
Until the woman lets you in

'Woman, let me in
Let me bring in the memories

Woman, let me in
Let me bring in the Devil Dreams'

I will not let you in
Don't you bring back the reveries
I turn into a bird
Carry further than the word is heard

'Woman, let me in
I'll turn into the wind
I'll blow you a cold kiss
Stronger than the song's hit'

I will not let you in
I face towards the wind
I change into the Mule . . .
'Let me in'
Hee – Haw
Hee – 'Haw
Hee – Haw
Hee – Haw
Hee – Haw
Hee – Haw
Hee – Haw'

Is that the wind from the Desert Song?

Is that an autumn leaf falling?

Or is that you walking home?

Never Be Mine

I look at you and see
My life that might have been
Your face just ghostly in the smoke
They're setting fire to the cornfields
As you're taking me home
The smell of burning fields
Will now mean you and here

This is where I want to be
This is what I need
This is where I want to be
This is what I need
This is where I want to be
But I know that this will never be mine

Ooh, the thrill and the hurting
The thrill and the hurting
I know that this will never be mine

I want you as the dream
Not the reality
That clumsy goodbye kiss could fool me
But I'm looking back over my shoulder
At you, happy without me

This is where I want to be
This is what I need
This is where I want to be
This is what I need

This is where I want to be
But I know that this will never be mine

Ooh, the thrill and the hurting
Will never be mine
The thrill and the hurting
It will never be mine
It can never be
The thrill and the hurting
Will never be mine

Why Should I Love You?

This chapter says
'Put it out of your mind'
Mmm, give it time . . .

The fine purple
The purest gold
The red of the Sacred Heart
The grey of a ghost
The 'L' of the lips are open
To the 'O' of the Host
The 'V' of the velvet

Of all of the people in the world
Why should I love you?
There's just something 'bout you
There's just something 'bout you
Of all the people in the world
Why should I love you?

Have you ever seen a picture
Of Jesus laughing?
Mmm, do you think
He had a beautiful smile?
A smile that healed

Of all the people in the world
Why should I love you?
There's just something 'bout you
There's just something 'bout you
Of all the people in the world

Why should I love you?
Of all the people in the world
Why should I love you?

The fine purple
The purest gold
The red of the Sacred Heart
The grey of a ghost
The 'L' of the lips are open
To the 'O' of the Host
The 'V' of the velvet
The 'E' of my eye
The eye in wonder
The eye that sees
The 'I' that loves you

Of all the people in the world
Why should I love you?

The Man with the Child in His Eyes

I hear him before I go to sleep
And focus on the day that's been
I realise he's there when I turn the light off
And turn over
Nobody knows about my man
They think he's lost on some horizon
And suddenly I find myself
Listening to a man I've never known before
Telling me about the sea
All his love, 'til eternity

Ooh he's here again –
The man with the child in his eyes

He's very understanding
And he's so aware of all my situations
And when I stay up late
He's always waiting
but I feel him hesitate
Oh, I'm so worried about my love
They say, 'No, no, it won't last forever'
And here I am again my girl
Wondering what on earth I'm doing here
Maybe he doesn't love me
I just took a trip on my love for him

Ooh he's here again –
The man with the child in his eyes

Reaching Out

See how the child reaches out instinctively
To feel how fire will feel

See how the man reaches out instinctively
For what he cannot have

The pull and the push of it all

Reaching out for the hand
Reaching out for the hand that smacked
Reaching out for that hand to hold
Reaching out for the Star
Reaching out for the Star that explodes
Reaching out for Mama

See how the flower leans instinctively toward the light
See how the heart reaches out instinctively
For no reason but to touch

The pull and the push of it all

Reaching out for the hand
Reaching out for the hand that smacked
Reaching out for that hand to hold
Reaching out for the Star
Reaching out for the Star that explodes
Reaching out for Mama

In Search of Peter Pan

It's been such a long week,
So much crying
I no longer see a future
I've been told, when I get older
That I'll understand it all
But I'm not sure if I want to
Running into her arms
At the school gates
She whispers that I'm a poor kid,
And granny takes me on her knee
She tells me I'm too sensitive
She makes me sad
She makes me feel like an old man
She makes me feel like an old man
They took the game right out of it
They took the game right out of it
When, when I am a man
I will be an astronaut
And find Peter Pan

Second Star on the right
Straight on 'til morning
Second Star on the right
Straight on 'til morning

Dennis loves to look in the mirror,
He tells me that he is beautiful
So I look too, and what do I see?
My eyes are full
But my face is empty

He's got a photo
Of his hero
He keeps it under his pillow
But I've got a pin-up
from a newspaper
Of Peter Pan
I found it in a locket
I hide it in my pocket
They took the game right out of it
They took the game right out of it
When, when I am a man
I will be an astronaut
And find Peter Pan

Second Star on the right
Straight on 'til morning
Second Star on the right
Straight on 'til morning
Second Star on the right
Straight on 'til morning

Rocket's Tail

That November night, looking up into the sky
You said, 'Hey, wish that was me up there
It's the biggest rocket I could find
And it's holding the night in its arms
If only for a moment.
I can't see the look in its eyes
But I'm sure it must be laughing'
But it seemed to me the saddest thing I'd ever seen
And I thought you were crazy wishing such a thing

I saw only a stick on fire
Alone on its journey
Home to the quickening ground
With no-one there to catch it

I put on my pointed hat
And my black and silver suit
And I check my gunpowder pack
And I strap the stick on my back
And dressed as a rocket on Waterloo Bridge
Nobody seems to see me
Then with the fuse in my hand
And now shooting into the night
And still as a rocket
I land in the river . . .

Was it me said you were crazy?

I put on my cloudiest suit
Size five lightning boots too

'Cause I am a rocket
On fire
Look at me go with my tail on fire
With my tail on fire
On fire
Hey, look at me go, look at me . . .
On fire

Night of the Swallow

The night doesn't like it
Looks just like your face
On the moon, to me
And I won't let you do
What you want to do
It's funny how, even now
You're laughing
I won't let you do it

If you go, I'll let the law know
And they'll head you off when you touch the ground
Ooh please
Don't go through with this
I don't like the sound of it
It's funny how, even now
You're miles away
I won't let you do it
I won't let you do it
I won't let you go through with it

'Meet them over at Dover
I'll just pilot the motor
Take them over the water

With a hired 'plane
And no names mentioned
Tonight's the night of the flight
Before you know
I'll be over the water like a swallow
There's no risk

I'll whisk them up
In no moonlight
And though pigs can fly
They'll never find me
Posing as the night
And I'm home before the morning'

In Malta, catch a swallow
For all of the guilty to let them free
Wings fill the window
And they beat and bleed
They hold the sky
On the other side
Of border lines
I won't let you do it
I won't let you do it
I won't let you go through with it

'Meet them over at Dover,
I'll just pilot the motor,
Take them over the water,
Like a swallow flying to Malta

With a hired 'plane
And no names mentioned
Tonight's the night of the flight
Before you know
I'll be over the water like a swallow
There's no risk
I'll whisk them up

In no moonlight
And though pigs can fly
They'll never find me
Posing as the night
And I'm home before the morning

Give me a break
Ooh let me fly
Give me something to show
For my miserable life
Give me something to take
Would you break even my wings
Like a swallow?
Let me, let me go

With a hired 'plane
And no names mentioned
Tonight's the night of the flight
Before you know
I'll be over the water like a swallow
There's no risk
I'll whisk them up
In no moonlight
And though pigs can fly
They'll never find me
Posing as the night
And I'm home before the morning'

But you're not a swallow

Home for Christmas

You know that I'll be waiting
To hear your footsteps saying
That you'll be coming home for Christmas

Please say you won't forget me
That every moment's empty

But only 'til you're coming home for Christmas
If only I had wings
Then I would fly to you
Through all the snowy weather
We'd be together
No-one makes me feel the way you do

You know that I'll be waiting
To hear your footsteps saying
That you'll be coming home
Home for Christmas

Moments of Pleasure

Some moments that I've had
Some moments of pleasure

I think about us lying
Lying on a beach somewhere
I think about us diving
Diving off a rock, into another moment

The case of George the Wipe
Oh God I can't stop laughing
This sense of humour of mine
It isn't funny at all
Oh but we sit up all night
Talking about it

Just being alive it can really hurt
And these moments given are a gift from time

On a balcony in New York
It's just started to snow
He meets us at the lift
Like Douglas Fairbanks
Waving his walking stick
But he isn't well at all
The buildings of New York
Look just like mountains
Through the snow

Just being alive it can really hurt
And these moments given are a gift from time
Just let us try to give these moments back
To those we love, to those who will survive

And I can hear my mother saying
'Every old sock meets an old shoe'
Isn't that a great saying?
'Every old sock meets an old shoe'
Here come the Hills of Time

Hey there, Maureen

Hey there, Bubba
Dancing down the aisle of a 'plane

s'Murph, playing his guitar refrain

Hey there, Teddy
Spinning in the chair at Abbey Road

Hey there, Bill
Could you turn the lights up?

Hey there, Michael
Do you really love me?

Did you really love me?

Is that a Storm

In the Swimming pool?

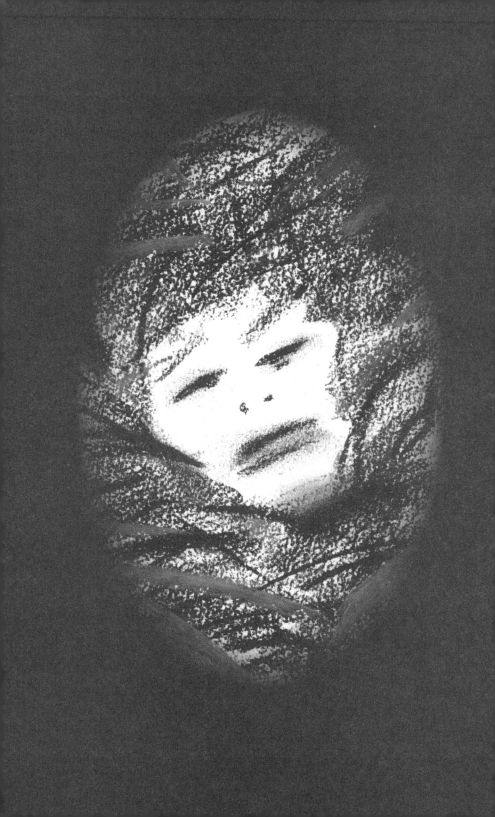

THE NINTH WAVE

And Dream of Sheep

Little light shining
Little light will guide them to me
My face is all lit up
My face is all lit up
If they find me racing white horses
They'll not take me for a buoy

Let me be weak, let me sleep and dream of sheep

Oh I'll wake up to any sound of engines
Every gull a seeking craft
I can't keep my eyes open
Wish I had my radio

I'd tune in to some friendly voices
Talking 'bout stupid things
I can't be left to my imagination
Let me be weak, let me sleep and dream of sheep

Ooh, their breath is warm
And they smell like sleep
And they say they take me home
Like poppies, heavy with seed
They take me deeper and deeper . . .

Under Ice

It's wonderful
Everywhere
So white
The river has frozen over
Not a soul
On the ice
Only me
Skating fast
I'm speeding past trees leaving
Little lines
In the ice
Cutting out
Little lines
In the ice, splitting
Splitting sound
Silver heels spitting
Spitting snow
There's something moving under
Under the ice
Moving under ice
Through water
Trying to get out of the cold water
It's me
Something, someone – help them
It's me

YOU **MUST** WAKE UP

Good morning de[c]

This is yo[

wake up

Wake up child

wAKE UP
LoVE

COME ON
WAKE UP

STOP YOUR LYING AND
STINKING IN BED
GET UP!

little light

Can you not see th[

Where?

There . . .

Where?

You still
in bed?

DON'T YOU **KNOW** YOU'[

KEP[

Wake up!

ly morning call

Wake up man

y att**EN**tion!

You should make the
night but see your little
light's **alight**

c'**MON** GET YOUR**S**ELF
OUT OF **THAT** BED!

e light **up there ?**

OVER **HERE**

wake up, sleepy head

AITING?

Look who's **here** to see **you** . . .

Waking the Witch

Listen to me, listen to me
Help me, help me, baby
Talk to me, talk to me
Please, please talk to me

'You won't burn'
Red, red roses
'You won't bleed'
Pinks and posies
'Confess to me, girl'
Red, red roses – go down

Spiritus Sanctus in nomine no-no-no-no
Spiritus Sanctus in nomine no-no-no-no

'Poor little thing'
Red, red roses
'The blackbird'
Pinks and posies
'Wings in the water –'
Red, red roses –
'Go down'
Pinks and posies

Deus et Dei Domino no-no-no-no
Deus et Dei Domino no-no-no-no

'What is it, child?'
Bless me, Father, bless me, Father, for I have sinned

Help me, baby, listen to me, listen to me
Tell them, baby, help me, baby, talk to them

'I question your innocence
She's a witch!'
Help this blackbird, there's a stone around my leg
'Uh, damn you, woman!'
Help this blackbird, there's a stone around my leg
'What say you, good people?'
'Guilty, Guilty, Guilty'
Help this blackbird –
'I am responsible for your actions'
'That Proves It'
Help this blackbird!
'Wake the witch'

Get out of the waves
*   Get out of the water*

Watching You Without Me

You can't hear me
You can't hear me
You can't hear what I'm saying
You can't hear what I'm saying to you

You watch the clock
Move the slow hand
I should have been home hours ago
But I'm not here, but I'm not here

You can't hear me
You can't hear me
You can't feel me
Here in the room with you now
You can't hear what I'm saying
You don't hear what I'm saying, do you?

Can't let you know
What's been happening
There's a ghost in our home
Just watching you without me
I'm not here, but I'm not here, but I'm not here

Don't ignore, don't ignore me
Let me in and don't be long

Don't ignore, don't ignore me
Let me in and don't be long

You can't hear me
You can't hear what I'm saying

You didn't hear me come in

**Help me, baby, help me, baby
Don't do this to me, baby
Listen to me, listen to me
Talk to me, talk to me, please**

**Listen to me, listen to me
Help me, help me, baby
Talk to me, talk to me
Please, please talk to me**

You won't hear me leaving

Jig of Life

Hello old lady
I know your face well
I know it well
She says, 'Ooh-na-na-na-na
I'll be sitting in your mirror
Now is the place where the crossroads meet
Will you look into the future

Never, never say goodbye
To my part of your life
No, no, no
Oh, oh, oh
Let me live'
She said, 'C'mon let me live'
She said, 'C'mon let me live, girl

'This moment in time
It doesn't belong to you
It belongs to me
And to your little boy and to your little girl
And the one hand clapping
Where on your palm is my little line
When you're written in mine
As an old memory?
Ooh-na-na-na-na-na

Never, never, never say goodbye
To my part of your life
No, no, no, no
Never, never, never, never

Let me go'
She said, 'C'mon let me live, girl'
She said, 'C'mon let me live, girl'

I put this moment . . .

                             here

I put this moment . . .

                    here

I put this moment . . .
over here

          over here!

Hello Earth

Hello Earth
Hello Earth
With just one hand held up high
I can blot you out
Out of sight
Peek-a-boo
Peek-a-boo, Little Earth
With just my heart and my mind
I can be driving
Driving home
And you asleep on the seat

I get out of my car
Step into the night
And look up at the sky
And there's something bright
Travelling fast
Just look at it go
Just look at it go

Hello Earth
Hello Earth
Watching storms
Start to form
Over America
Can't do anything
Just watch them swing
With the wind
Out to sea
All you sailors

Get out of the waves, get out of the water
All life-savers
Get out of the waves, get out of the water
All you cruisers
Get out of the waves, get out of the water
All you fishermen
Head for home
Go to sleep, Little Earth

I was there at the birth
Out of the cloud burst the head of the Tempest
Murderer, Murderer of calm
Why did I go?
Why did I go?

Go to sleep, Little Earth

The Morning Fog

The light
Begin to bleed
Begin to breathe
Begin to speak
D'you know what?
I love you better now

I am falling
Like a stone
Like a storm
Being born again
Into the sweet morning fog
D'you know what?
I love you better now

I am falling
And I'd love to hold you now
I'll kiss the ground
I'll tell my mother
I'll tell my father
I'll tell my loved one
I'll tell my brothers
How much I love them

And think inside out
You jump 'round three times
You jump into the mirror...

How To Be Invisible

I found a book on how to be invisible
Take a pinch of keyhole
And fold yourself up
You cut along the dotted line
You think inside out
And you're invisible

Eye of Braille
Hem of Anorak
Stem of Wallflower
Hair of Doormat

I found a book on how to be invisible
On the edge of the Labyrinth
Under a veil you must never lift
Pages you must never turn
In the Labyrinth

You stand in front of a million doors
And each one holds a million more
Corridors that lead to the World
Of the Invisible
Corridors that twist and turn
Corridors that blister and burn

Eye of Braille
Hem of Anorak
Stem of Wallflower
Hair of Doormat

Is that the wind from the Desert Song?
Is that an autumn leaf falling?
Or is that you walking home?
Is that the wind from the Desert Song?
Is that an autumn leaf falling?
Or is that you walking home?
Is that a Storm in the Swimming pool?

You take a pinch of keyhole
And fold yourself up
You cut along the dotted line
And think inside out
You jump 'round three times
You jump into the mirror
And you're invisible

50 Words for Snow

1 drifting
2 twisting
3 whiteout
4 blackbird braille
5 Wenceslasaire
6 avalanche

Come on, man, you've got 44 to go, come on man you've got
  44 to go. Come on man, you've got
44 to go, come on man, you've got 44 to go

 7 swans-a-melting
 8 deamondi-pavlova
 9 eiderfalls
10 Santanyeroofdikov
11 stellatundra
12 hunter's dream
13 faloop'njoompoola
14 zebranivem
15 spangladasha
16 albadune
17 hironocrashka
18 hooded-wept

Come on, Joe, you've got 32 to go, come on, Joe
you've got 32 to go. Come on now, you've got 32 to go, come
  on now, you've got 32 to go
Don't you know it's not just the Eskimo?
Let me hear your 50 words for snow

19   phlegm de neige
20   mountainsob
21   anklebreaker
22   erase-o-dust
23   shnamistoflopp'n
24   terrablizza
25   whirlissimo
26   vanilla swarm
27   icyskidski
28   robber's veil

Come on, Joe, just 22 to go, come on, Joe
just 22 to go. Come on, Joe, just you and the Eskimos. Come
    on now, just 22 to go. Come on now
just 22 to go, let me hear your 50 words for snow

29   creaky-creaky
30   psychohail
31   whippoccino
32   shimmerglisten
33   Zhivagodamarbletasl
34   sorbetdeluge
35   sleetspoot'n
36   melt-o-blast
37   slipperella
38   boomerangablanca
39   groundberry down
40   meringuerpeaks
41   crème-bouffant
42   peDtaH 'ej chIS qo'

Lyra

Where are our lives?
If there is no dream
Where is our home?
We don't know how
There will be a way
Out of the storm
We will find home

And her soul walks beside her
An army stands behind her
Lyra, Lyra

And her face – full of grace
Two worlds collide around her
The truth lies deep inside her
Lyra, Lyra

And the stars look down upon her
As darkness settles on her
Lyra, Lyra

Who's to know what's in the future?
But we hope we will be with her
We have all our love to give her
Lyra, Lyra

And her soul walks beside her
An army stands behind her
Lyra, Lyra

And her face – full of grace
Two worlds collide around her
The truth lies deep inside her
Lyra, Lyra

Mother Stands for Comfort

She knows that I've been doing something wrong
But she won't say anything
She thinks that I was with my friends yesterday
But she won't mind me lying
Mmh because:

Mother stands for comfort
Mother will hide the murderer

It breaks the cage, fear escapes and takes possession
Just like a crowd rioting inside –
Make me do this, make me do that, make me do this
Make me do that –
Am I the cat that takes the bird?
To her the hunted, not the hunter.

Mother stands for comfort
Mother will hide the murderer
Mother hides the madman
Mother will stay Mum
Mother stands for comfort
Mother will stay Mum
She stands for comfort

Mrs Bartolozzi

I remember it was that Wednesday
Oh when it rained and it rained
They traipsed mud all over the house
It took hours and hours to scrub it out
All over the hall carpet
I took my mop and my bucket
And I cleaned and I cleaned
The kitchen floor
Until it sparkled
Then I took my laundry basket
And put all the linen in it
And everything I could fit in it
All our dirty clothes that hadn't gone into the wash
And all your shirts and jeans and things
And put them in the new washing machine
Washing machine
Washing machine

I watched them going 'round and 'round
My blouse wrapping itself around your trousers
Oh the waves are going out
My skirt floating up around my waist
As I wade out into the surf
Oh and the waves are coming in
Oh and the waves are going out
Oh and you're standing right behind me
Little fish swim between my legs
Oh and the waves are coming in
Oh and the waves are going out
Oh and the waves are coming in

Out of the corner of my eye
I think I see you standing outside
But it's just your shirt
Hanging on the washing line
Waving its arm as the wind blows by
And it looks so alive
Nice and white
Just like it's climbed right out
of my washing machine
Washing machine
Washing machine

Slooshy sloshy slooshy sloshy
Get that dirty shirty clean
Slooshy sloshy slooshy sloshy
Make those cuffs and collars gleam
Everything clean and shiny

Washing machine?
Washing machine!
Washing machine

Wuthering Heights

Out on the wiley, windy moors
We'd roll and fall in green
You had a temper, like my jealousy
Too hot, too greedy
How could you leave me?
When I needed to possess you
I hated you, I loved you, too

Bad dreams in the night
They told me I was going to lose the fight
Leave behind my wuthering, wuthering
Wuthering Heights

Heathcliff, it's me, Cathy, come home
I'm so cold, let me in your window

Oh it gets dark, it gets lonely
On the other side from you
I pine alot, I find the lot
Falls through without you
I'm coming back, love, cruel Heathcliff
My one dream, my only master

Too long I roam in the night
I'm coming back to his side, to put it right
I'm coming home to wuthering, wuthering
Wuthering Heights

Oh let me have it, let me grab your soul away
Oh let me have it, let me grab your soul away

You know it's me, Cathy

Heathcliff, it's me, Cathy, come home
I'm so cold, let me in your window

This Woman's Work

Pray God you can cope
I stand outside this woman's work
This woman's world
Ooh, it's hard on the man
Now his part is over
Now starts the craft of the father

I know you have a little life in you yet
I know you have a lot of strength left
I know you have a little life in you yet
I know you have a lot of strength left

I should be crying but I just can't let it show
I should be hoping but I can't stop thinking
Of all the things I should've said
That I never said
All the things we should've done
That we never did
All the things I should've given
But I didn't
Oh, darling, make it go
Make it go away

Give me these moments back
Give them back to me
Give me that little kiss
Give me your hand

I know you have a little life in you yet
I know you have a lot of strength left

I know you have a little life in you yet
I know you have a lot of strength left

I should be crying but I just can't let it show
I should be hoping but I can't stop thinking
Of all the things we should've said
That were never said
All the things we should've done
That we never did
All the things that you needed from me
All the things that you wanted for me
All the things I should've given
But I didn't
Oh, darling, make it go away
Just make it go away now

Lake Tahoe

Lake Tahoe
Cold mountain water. Don't ever swim there.
Just stand on the edge and look in there
And you might see a woman down there
They say some days, up she comes, up she rises
As if out of nowhere
Wearing Victorian dress
She was calling her pet
'Snowflake! Snowflake!'
Tumbling like a cloud that has drowned in the lake

Just like a poor, porcelain doll . . .
Her eyes are open but no-one's home
The clock has stopped
So long she's gone
No-one's home
Her old dog is sleeping
His legs are frail now
But when he dreams
He runs . . .
Along long beaches and sticky fields
Through the Spooky Wood looking for her

The beds are made. The table is laid. The door is open –
Someone is calling:
It's a woman
'Here boy, here boy! You've come home!
I've got an old bone and a biscuit and so much love
Miss me? Did you miss me?
Here's the kitchen – There's your basket

Here's the hall – That's where you wait for me
Here's the bedroom – You're not allowed in there
Here's my lap – That's where you lay your head   .
Here boy, oh you're a good boy
You've come home
You've come home
You've come home!'

…And you're invisible